Deck
The Halls

Quilts to

Celebrate Christmas

CHERYL ALMGREN TAYLOR

Martingale®
& COMPANY

Deck the Halls:
Quilts to Celebrate Christmas
© 2009 by Cheryl Almgren Taylor

 *Martingale*®
& COMPANY

That Patchwork Place® is an imprint
of Martingale & Company®.

Martingale & Company
20205 144th Avenue NE
Woodinville, WA 98072-8478
www.martingale-pub.com

Printed in China
14 13 12 11 10 09   8 7 6 5 4 3

Library of Congress Cataloging-in-Publication Data
Library of Congress Control Number: 2009013170

ISBN: 978-1-56477-910-6

Credits

President & CEO Tom Wierzbicki

Editor in Chief Mary V. Green

Managing Editor Tina Cook

Developmental Editor Karen Costello Soltys

Technical Editor Laurie Baker

Copy Editor Melissa Bryan

Design Director Stan Green

Production Manager Regina Girard

Illustrator Laurel Strand

Cover Designer Stan Green

Text Designer Regina Girard

Photographer Brent Kane

Mission Statement

Dedicated to providing quality products
and service to inspire creativity.

Dedication

To my husband, Kenny, who is the most wonderful husband in the world. Thank you for your encouragement, praise, advice, and support in everything I do. Thank you for waiting on benches as I shop for fabric, for running out at all hours to buy a supply I need, and for driving miles out of our way to visit one more quilt store. Thank you for your patience and strength. You are a wonderful man, and I love you with all my heart.

And to Debbie Lindgren, without whom I would never have become a published quilt designer. Thank you for your insistence that I submit a proposal to a publisher, your quilting advice and expertise, your generosity, and your friendship. Everyone should be so blessed as to have a friend like you.

Acknowledgments

I would like to extend my thanks to the following people for their help and support in my quilting and designing:

To Mary Green, Karen Soltys, Laurie Baker, Cathy Reitan, and the many people at Martingale & Company who put my designs into print. Thank you for your help and support during the publishing process and for your belief in my ability.

To Mary Kay Fields, my shop-hop partner and good friend. Thank you for sharing your vast store of quilting knowledge and expertise and for sewing those last-minute bindings.

To the "Quilters of Faith" of Western Hills Christian Church—Linda, Marcia, Irene, and Nicci—thank you for testing my patterns and for all the fun we have together.

To Cheryl Winslow of Starshine Quilting. Thank you for the stunning quilting and for laboring through the night to meet my deadlines. Your work is wonderful!

And to Jane Garrison and YLI Thread Corporation, thanks for providing the beautiful threads used to sew these quilts.

CONTENTS

INTRODUCTION

*Christmas is my favorite holiday, and every year as the season
draws near I have the desire to make quilts for friends and family.*

When I make a quilt for someone, whether the recipient realizes it or not, I am giving a part of myself—with each stitch I take, a part of my heart goes into the quilt. I have loved creating this collection of quilts for the Christmas season, putting myself into each design. I hope that as you read through the pages, you will find quilts that speak to your heart, from mine.

In my designing career, and especially as I worked on this book, I have learned several things about myself. One is that I love appliqué. I love the shapes and the graceful curves you can create, as well as the flexibility the technique provides. I have also learned that I love intricate designs. My husband often laughs at me when I try to create a simple project, because I always want to add one or two more details, just a little something more to make it extra special. But not all quilters are like me, and I have tried to remember that as I worked on *Deck the Halls*.

In this book I have attempted to provide a little something for everyone. There is an abundance of appliqué, from the simple shapes in "Pretty Poinsettias Quilt" (page 31) to the intricate designs of "Pomegranates and Posies Quilt" (page 45). There is also a project, "Peppermint Candy Table Runner" (page 55), that is entirely pieced. It uses quick and easy sewing for those who want something simple.

"Cleone's Christmas Stocking" (page 75) is a project that even a beginning quilter can complete with ease. I modeled it after the Christmas stockings my mother made for my sister and me when we were very small. Both my sister and my mother passed away many years ago, but this simple little stocking makes them a part of my Christmas celebration today.

There are several projects to brighten your holiday table and others that will bring color and fun into your Christmas decor. "Yuletide Ornaments Mantel Runner" (page 37) will grace your mantelpiece with garlands even if you have no greenery, and you can hang "Christmas Kisses Quilt" (page 89) even if you have no mistletoe.

I hope this collection of designs helps you create beautiful quilts that friends and family members will treasure in their holiday celebrations. I hope it causes you, also, to reflect on the wonder and magnitude of the gift the world received at the first Christmas. May your Christmas be filled with joy . . . and quilts!

~Cheryl

TOOLS AND SUPPLIES

Having the right equipment for the job, whether you are creating a quilt or remodeling your house, makes the entire experience quicker and more pleasant.

FABRIC

When I make a quilt, my fabric of choice is always 100% cotton. It is easy to work with and presses beautifully. The array of gorgeous cotton fabrics available from quality manufacturers is amazing, and you can find almost any type of print or design you could want.

Having said that, this is a book of Christmas quilts and sometimes a girl wants a little glitz and glitter at the holidays. My family often jokes about my love of bright, shiny objects. Many manufacturers create 100%-cotton Christmas fabrics with metallic designs and glitter elements. These are usually as easy to work with as any other cotton fabric.

If you want something even more shiny and eye-catching, it is possible to use small amounts of special-occasion fabrics—such as those designed for bridal gowns, prom dresses, and dance costumes—in your appliqué successfully. Just remember to read the manufacturer's information carefully. It is highly probable that the fabric will not be washable. Also, check the temperature of your iron when pressing specialty fabrics. They usually require a much lower heat setting than cotton. Press them cautiously; some types of glittering fabrics have been known to melt at the touch of the iron. If this all sounds alarming, you might forgo the use of specialty fabrics and instead use metallic threads in your quilting to add a hint of pizzazz.

THREAD

The quantity and variety of threads available to quilters today is overwhelming. Different threads are designed for different needs and provide different results, so when selecting your thread, you need to know the look you want to achieve in your completed project. Keep in mind that the higher the number, the finer the thread.

Threads for Piecing

If you are using cotton fabric, I recommend 50- or 60-weight, 100%-cotton thread for piecing. When I first began quilting, I used 50-weight cotton exclusively, but recently I have found that 60-weight cotton reduces the bulk in the seams and helps the pieces lie flatter. It also improves the accuracy of the finished-size piece. Experiment with the threads you have, because a few 50-weight brands also provide these results.

Threads for Appliqué

Most of the projects in this book feature fusible appliqué. With this technique, the thread used to finish the edge of the appliqués becomes an important design element that affects the look of your finished project. If you want a primitive look or you like to draw attention to the thread, use 40- or 50-weight cotton. A heavier weight or specialty thread can also achieve this look. Rayon threads provide a soft luster that highlights the appliqué. If you want a soft, subtle look with a little sheen, silk thread provides a beautiful finish.

Many quilters prefer the look of needle-turn appliqué but use fusible-web techniques to save time. If this is you, stitch around your appliqués with 60-weight cotton thread in a color that matches your fabric; this will camouflage your fused edges from a distance. Or, if you don't want the thread to be seen at all, use a good-quality .004 invisible monofilament thread and a narrow stitch width.

SEWING MACHINE

Make sure your sewing machine is in good working order and has received any necessary servicing before you begin to sew. For piecing, you will need a straight stitch, which is basic on all sewing machines. For machine quilting, you'll need a walking foot and/or a darning foot. If you enjoy fusible-web appliqué, it is nice to have a machine with a blanket stitch, but if yours does not have this, you can use a zigzag stitch instead. If you have an array of fancy stitches, you may want to experiment with designs to use on your appliqué edges.

SEWING-MACHINE NEEDLES

Be sure to select the appropriate needle for your thread and technique, and change your needle after several hours of use. Specialty needles are designed for different types of threads and different purposes. For piecing and appliqué, I usually use a size 75/11 Sharp needle, but a size 70/10 or 80/12 can also be a good choice depending on the size of thread you are using. For machine quilting, use needles specifically created for machine quilting; they're designed to go through several layers of fabric and sew evenly over seams. Do not use a universal needle for piecing or quilting because its rounded tip doesn't produce the nice, even stitches that a Sharp does.

ROTARY-CUTTING TOOLS

To cut fabrics for piecing, you will need a rotary cutter, a rotary-cutting mat, and clear acrylic rulers. Purchase the largest rotary-cutting mat that your quilting space can accommodate. If you don't already have a selection of rotary cutters, start with one that has a 45 mm blade, as this is the most versatile. Change the blades in your cutter when they become dull. Always, always, *always* use extreme caution when using the rotary cutter. Do not use one while sitting down—a little lesson I learned after a quick trip to the emergency room to reattach my fingertip. Treat this tool with extreme respect!

Because of a previous hand injury (not caused by a rotary cutter), I prefer acrylic rulers designed to grip fabric. A 6" x 24" ruler and a 6" square are often recommended for beginners, but an 8½" x 24" ruler and a 6½" square provide some extra size that is useful. A 15" square ruler is also nice for squaring up your quilt.

SCISSORS

In quilting and sewing, it is essential that you have two types of scissors—one for cutting paper and one for cutting fabric. Don't ever let anyone use your fabric shears on a piece of paper. Husbands and children must be trained early on to know the difference. If you can afford it, buy a quality pair of fabric shears, and if you enjoy appliqué, purchase a pair of small, sharp-pointed fabric scissors for cutting intricate pieces as well.

FUSIBLE WEB

There are a number of fusible-web products available that come in various weights and are designed for use with different materials. For fusible-web appliqué, you will want to purchase a lightweight, paper-backed fusible web designed to be used with fabric. Some of the trade names include HeatnBond, Wonder-Under, and Steam-A-Seam. You will need a product that is specifically labeled "lightweight." The medium- and heavyweight products will make your quilt stiff and bulky. Be aware that the lightweight products will not permanently attach your appliqué to the quilt. The web temporarily attaches the appliqué pieces, but the edges will need to be permanently secured using a blanket stitch, zigzag stitch, or other decorative stitch.

IRON

A good iron is important in quilting and essential for successful fusible-web appliqué. Be sure to keep your iron clean and watch for pieces of fusible web that might adhere to the bottom. My husband prefers to wear his shirts without brown, gunky fusible-web residue, as he has mentioned to me on more than one occasion.

TEFLON PRESSING SHEET

Although you may be able to get by without one, a Teflon pressing sheet is a great asset when using fusible web. It enables you to preassemble appliqué pieces easily before adhering them to the quilt top, and it keeps the adhesive from melting onto your iron.

PINS

Fine silk pins are wonderful for use in piecing. You can purchase them with or without glass heads. Although they are a little more expensive, they slide easily into your fabric and are a pleasure to use. You will also need size 1 rustproof safety pins if you will be machine quilting your projects.

SEAM RIPPER

Buy yourself a sharp seam ripper and resign yourself to the fact that this tool is our friend. It is much better to rip, redo, and be proud of your project than to ignore a problem and be unhappy with the finished quilt.

QUILTMAKING BASICS

This section will cover all the techniques needed to make the quilts in this book.

ROTARY CUTTING

The rotary cutter is a terrific innovation that has revolutionized the quilt world. It allows us to execute quick, precise cutting that simply isn't possible with scissors. You will need to use the cutter with a 24"-long acrylic ruler, a small square ruler, and a rotary-cutting mat to protect your work surface.

1. Iron your fabric to remove any wrinkles. Fold it in half with the selvage edges together and lay it on the cutting mat, aligning the folded edge with a horizontal line of the mat. On the left edge of the fabric, place the square ruler along the fold and butt the 24" ruler against the left edge of the square so that it covers ¼" to ½" of the raw edges.

2. With your hand on the long ruler to prevent shifting, remove the small square ruler. Roll the rotary cutter along the right edge of the ruler across the width of the fabric. Never cut toward yourself; always cut away. Discard the uneven scrap. You now have a straight edge from which to cut your strips.

3. Align the ruler at the desired measurement along the edge of the fabric. Make sure that the ruler marking is on the top edge of the fabric and not beside it, which would make your fabric strip too small. Cut along the ruler edge toward the selvage. Repeat the process for the necessary amount of strips.

4. After cutting several strips, it may be necessary to straighten the edge of the fabric again. Repeat steps 1 and 2 to do this, and then continue cutting your required strips.

5. Squares and rectangles can now be cut from the strips. Trim away the selvage ends of the folded strip in the same way that you trimmed the fabric piece in steps 1 and 2. Measure the required distance from the straightened ends of the strip and cut the pieces. You will be cutting two pieces at once.

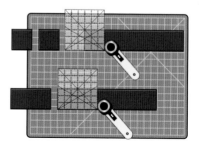

Fusible-Web Appliqué

Appliqué is the process of sewing fabric shapes to a background fabric, enabling the quilter to create designs that are not possible with traditional piecing. There are many appliqué techniques, some that have been around for hundreds of years and some that are relatively recent. These include needle turning, using freezer-paper templates, spray starch and pressing, and basting the fabric edges. Many books are available that teach these methods, but in this book I concentrate on fusible-web appliqué, which differs from other techniques in several ways.

When working with fusible-web appliqué, any shapes that are not symmetrical must be prepared in reverse, or as a mirror image, otherwise your finished design will be facing backward. In this book, the designs have already been reversed for you so that you do not need to do this step.

Using Fusible Web

Although several types of fusible web are available, I recommend a paper-backed, lightweight product. Be sure to read the manufacturer's instructions when applying fusible web to your fabrics, because each brand is a little different and requires a slightly different fusing time. Pressing too long may result in fusible web that doesn't stick well. In some geographical areas, excess humidity may cause the paper backing to separate from the fusible web and become difficult to use. If you encounter this problem, try a different brand.

1. Trace the pattern directly onto the paper side of the fusible web. You may find it helpful to use a light box if you have one.

TRACING MULTIPLES

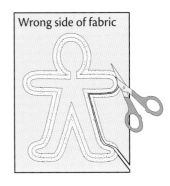

If you are tracing an appliqué shape that will need to be repeated multiple times, you may wish to use a template. For this method, trace the shape onto template plastic using a fine-tip permanent pen. Cut out the shape exactly on the drawn line. Use this piece as a template and trace around it onto the paper side of the fusible web until you have drawn the required number of shapes. This will ensure that all your pieces are identical.

2. Roughly cut out each shape, leaving about a ¼" margin around the outside of the traced line. To reduce stiffness in a medium- or large-sized appliqué shape, cut away the center portion of the paper-backed fusible web. Be sure to leave at least ¼" of paper inside the traced line.

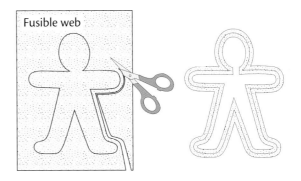

Fusible web

3. Follow the manufacturer's instructions to fuse each shape to the wrong side of the appropriate fabric, and then cut out the shape on the traced line. Don't remove the paper backing until you're ready to fuse the shape in place.

Wrong side of fabric

4. Remove the paper backing and position the shapes on the background piece in numerical order. A dotted line on a pattern indicates that a piece is underneath an adjacent piece. It is often helpful to use a placement guide for accuracy. Once you are sure everything is in the correct position, fuse the pieces in place.

5. Stitch around the edge of each appliqué using a machine blanket stitch, zigzag stitch, or satin stitch.

Preassembling Appliqué Units

When several appliqué pieces are needed to make a shape, such as the pomegranate in "Pomegranates and Posies Quilt," it is helpful to preassemble the pieces into a unit before fusing it to the background. A Teflon pressing sheet can be very useful for this because fusible web will not adhere to the sheet. If some glue does stick during the assembling process, let the sheet cool momentarily and then peel off the sticky residue. It's important that you remove any residue from the Teflon sheet when assembling pieces so that the wrong things don't get stuck together!

To preassemble an appliqué unit, prepare the shapes as instructed in "Using Fusible Web." Lay the appliqués on the pressing sheet in the order indicated on the placement guide. Remove the paper backing behind the areas that overlap another appliqué shape, and then fuse the pieces together. Keep the rest of the paper backing in place until you're ready to fuse the entire unit to the background fabric.

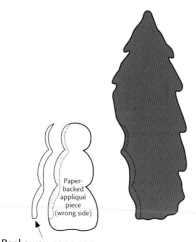

Paper-backed appliqué piece (wrong side)

Peel away paper on overlapping areas.

Making and Appliquéing Bias Vines

The projects "Yuletide Ornament Mantel Runner" and "Pomegranates and Posies Quilt" both use vines in their appliqué. Appliquéd vines are made from bias strips, which can be prepared and attached in one of several ways. It is possible to purchase bias bars to help in the construction of bias strips, but I prefer a different method.

Before preparing the vines, be sure to mark your fabric for the vine placement. You will use this line when you sew the vines to the quilt.

1. Refer to "Cutting and Joining Bias Strips" on page 16 to cut the required amount of strips. To make bias vines that are ¼" wide or less, cut the bias strips 1¼" wide. For wider vines, increase the width of the bias strips. Traditionally, bias strips are cut double the finished size *plus ½"*.

2. Sew the strips together as described. Press the long strip in half lengthwise, *wrong* sides together.

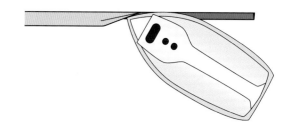

3. For ¼"-wide finished vines, sew ¼" from the fold (with the wrong sides still together). To make a narrower vine, sew closer to the fold. Trim the seam allowance to approximately ⅛".

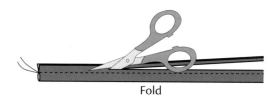

Fold

4. Align the raw edges of the bias strip along the marked pattern line. Make sure the bias strip is on the bottom side of the line, not the top. Stitch the bias strip in place, sewing on top of the existing stitches. Press the bias strip over the stitching, covering the raw edge.

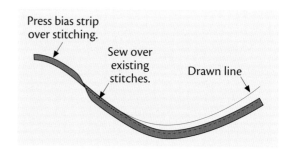

Press bias strip over stitching.

Sew over existing stitches.

Drawn line

5. Sew down the top edge of the bias strip. If you want both sides to look the same, topstitch the bottom edge of the bias strip as well.

Paper Piecing

Paper piecing is a method used in the border of "Christmas Kisses Quilt" and in the ornaments on "Yuletide Ornaments Mantel Runner." Although traditional piecing is an option for these areas, paper piecing will make it easier to handle the small pieces while ensuring accurate results.

It is possible to purchase paper specifically designed for paper piecing, but you can also use tracing paper or vellum paper. The paper needs to be easy to see through and it should tear away easily.

1. Transfer the pattern onto your paper foundation and make the required number of copies for the project. Be sure to transfer the numbers, which indicate the sewing order. Roughly cut around each foundation so that you can work on each one individually.

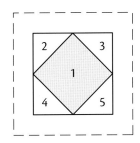

2. Set the stitch length on your sewing machine to 15 to 18 stitches per inch. You may also wish to use a larger needle size, such as 90/14. The smaller stitch length and larger needle will enable the paper to tear away easily when you are done.

3. Turn the foundation pattern so the marked side is facing up. Cut a piece of fabric for area 1 that is at least ¼" larger than the area on all sides. Position the fabric right side up over area 1, making sure it completely covers the area and extends ¼" past the lines on all sides. *When paper piecing, the fabric pieces must always extend at least ¼" past the lines, including those along the perimeter of the block. This is your seam-allowance fabric.*

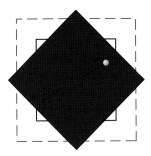

4. Cut a piece of fabric for area 2 and place it on the pattern to be sure that it covers the area with an ample ¼" seam allowance on all sides. Flip it over on top of fabric piece 1, right sides together, and pin it in place.

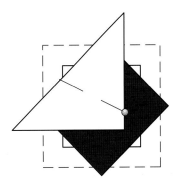

5. Flip the foundation pattern over so that the *unmarked* side is on top. You should be able to see the lines that are drawn on the other side. Position the unit under the presser foot, and sew exactly on the line between areas 1 and 2, starting and ending a few stitches past the line with a backstitch.

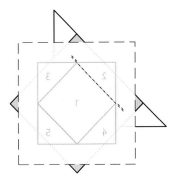

6. Turn the paper over and open piece 2. Press the piece in place, using a dry iron. Trim the seam allowance to ¼" if necessary, being careful not to cut into the paper.

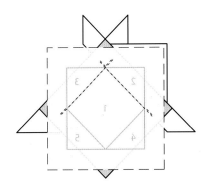

7. Continue cutting and adding fabric pieces to each area in order until the block is completed. After the blocks are assembled into the quilt, you will tear away the foundation paper. It is important to leave the foundation paper in place until each block is sewn to another piece, because some of the edges may be bias.

SQUARING UP BLOCKS

The backgrounds of appliqué blocks are oversized to allow for some distortion that occurs while appliqué-ing. Before assembling the quilt, you will need to trim the blocks to size.

1. Locate the center of the finished block, and then establish the midpoint of the block on a ruler. For example, on a block that is 6" square, the midpoint of the block is 3" down from the top and 3" in from the side. (This is a small block; depending on the actual size of your block, you may need to use more than one ruler.)

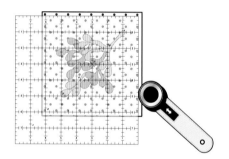

2. Place the ruler(s) on the block, aligning the center of the block and the midpoint on the ruler. Trim the excess fabric from one side.

3. Rotate the block and repeat step 2 for each of the remaining sides.

ADDING BORDERS

The projects in this book depict a variety of border types. Some of the quilts have pieced borders composed of blocks. Others have borders with butted corners, and a few feature mitered corners.

I recommend waiting to cut your borders until your quilt top is ready for them. Always measure through the *center* of the quilt when measuring for borders, as the sides of the quilt can easily become distorted during construction.

If your border length is longer than 40", you will need to piece the border strips to achieve the required length. When piecing border strips, use a diagonal seam. Trim the seam allowances to ¼" and press them open.

Borders with Butted Corners

1. Measure through the center of the quilt from top to bottom. Prepare two border strips to this measurement. Locate the center of the borders and the center of the quilt sides. Matching centers and ends, pin the borders to each side of the quilt, right sides together. Sew using a ¼" seam allowance. Press the seam allowances toward the border.

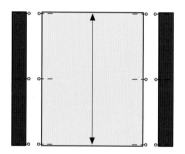

2. Measure through the center of the quilt from side to side, including the side borders. Prepare two border strips to this measurement. Mark the center of the borders and the center of the quilt top and bottom. Matching centers and ends, pin the borders to the top and bottom of the quilt, right sides together. Sew using a ¼" seam allowance. Press the seam allowances toward the border.

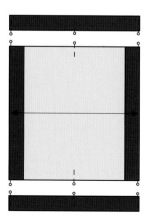

Borders with Mitered Corners

1. Determine the finished length of the side border strips and the top and bottom border strips. To do this, measure through the center of the quilt top in both directions. To these measurements, add twice the finished width of the border plus an additional 2" to 3". For example, if your quilt top measures 40" x 60" and the finished border width is 6", the cut length of the top and bottom border strips would be approximately 55" (40"+6"+6"+3") and the cut length of the side border strips would be approximately 75" (60"+6"+6"+3").

2. Pin-mark the center point on each edge of the quilt. Pin-mark the center and *finished* length on each border strip.

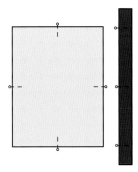

3. Measure and mark ¼" from each of the quilt-top corners.

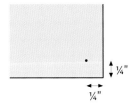

4. Pin the side borders to the quilt top, matching centers and the border end points to the quilt-top corner points. Sew the borders to the quilt top, beginning and ending at the ¼" marks. Repeat with the top and bottom borders.

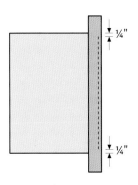

5. Lay your quilt on a large, flat surface, such as the top of an ironing board. Fold the quilt so that the borders at one corner are aligned, right sides together and edges even. Pin the borders together. Using a ruler, extend the folded line of the quilt onto the borders with a drawn pencil line. This will create a 45° stitching line.

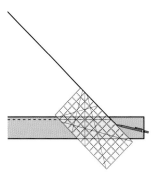

6. Machine baste on the drawn line, beginning at the corner dot and ending at the border edge. Open out the corner and check for accuracy. Adjust if necessary. If the corner is correct, stitch over the basting.

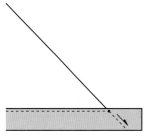

7. Trim the excess fabric, leaving a ⅜" seam allowance. Press the seam allowance open.

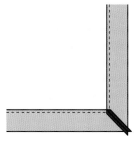

8. Repeat the process for the remaining three corners.

Binding

After the quilting is completed, you will need to bind the quilt edges. There are two types of binding used to finish a quilt: straight-grain binding and bias binding. Any quilt with curves or scalloped edges must be finished with a bias binding because a straight-grain binding will not curve without pleating. "Yuletide Ornaments Mantel Runner" (page 37) is an example of a project that requires bias binding, but I also recommend it for straight-edged quilts because it wears well and can add an interesting design element if you are using a striped or checked binding fabric. The only difference in assembling the two types of binding is how you cut the strips. After that, they are sewn together and attached to the quilt in the same manner.

Binding is traditionally ¼" to ⅜" finished, which requires cutting 2½"-wide strips, but you can make your binding wider or narrower according to personal taste. To determine how wide to cut your strips, multiply the desired finished binding width by six. The project instructions specify the number of widths to cut or the length of binding to assemble.

Cutting and Joining Bias Strips

1. To cut bias strips, open up your fabric and lay it flat on your cutting mat, right side up. Align the 45° line on your rotary-cutting ruler with one of the selvage edges. Cut along the ruler edge to make the first cut.

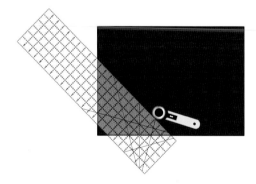

2. Using the first cut as a guide, align the desired strip-width measurement (usually 2½") on the ruler with the cut edge of the fabric. Cut along the edge of the ruler. Continue cutting strips until you have the quantity needed.

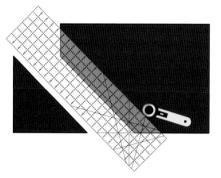

3. To join the strips, place the ends of two strips right sides together, forming an angle that looks like the bottom half of the letter X. The overlap of fabric strips creates a V on each side. Stitch between the two Vs. Press the seam allowance open and trim to ¼", if needed. Join the remaining strips in the same manner to make one long strip.

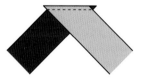

Cutting and Joining Straight-Grain Strips

1. Cut your fabric strips the width specified in the project instructions, cutting across the width of the fabric from selvage edge to selvage edge.

2. To join the strips, place the ends of two strips right sides together. Sew diagonally across the strip as shown. Trim the seam allowance to ¼" and press the seam allowance open. Join the remaining strips in the same manner to make one long strip.

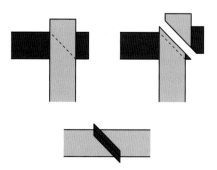

Attaching Binding

1. Trim the batting and backing even with the quilt top and square up the quilt. Be sure that the three layers of the quilt are basted together along the edges.

2. Press the binding strip in half lengthwise, wrong sides together and raw edges aligned.

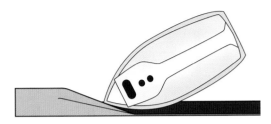

3. Beginning near the center of one edge, align the raw edges of the binding with the edge of the quilt top. Begin stitching about 8" from the end of the binding strip, using a ¼" seam allowance. Stop sewing ¼" from the corner. Backstitch, and remove the quilt from under the sewing machine.

Quilt top

8"

¼"

Binding strip

4. Fold the binding up to form a 45° angle. The binding edge should be aligned with the next side of the quilt.

5. Fold the binding back down on itself, leaving the 45° angle in place underneath. Align the binding and quilt edges and continue sewing, repeating the procedure at each corner.

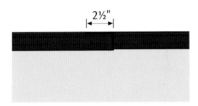

6. When you are approximately 8" from the beginning of the binding, overlap the beginning and end of the binding strip. Trim the end so that the overlap measures 2½" (the width of the binding strip).

2½"

7. Open up the folded binding and place the two ends right sides together. Mark a diagonal line on the wrong side. Sew the ends together on the line. Check to make sure the binding fits the quilt edge, and then trim the seam allowance to ¼" and press it open. Refold the binding and finish sewing it in place.

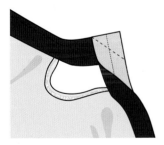

8. Fold the binding over the edge of the quilt to the back. Hand stitch it in place, forming miters at the corners.

Quilt back

CHRISTMAS IS COMING

*With Christmas coming, 'tis the season to bring a dash of extra joy
and excitement into your home. What better way to do
this than by creating a new quilt for your Christmas
celebration? Whether it's a door banner to welcome yuletide
carolers or a mantel scarf to grace the fireplace, quilts
offer a bounty of delightful ways to deck the halls.*

WELCOME CHRISTMAS DOOR BANNER

If you love Christmas as I do, the holiday actually begins weeks before December 25, as we open our homes and hearts to friends and family. Start the festive season by hanging this welcoming door banner to greet guests. The wintry scenes are created with a combination of piecing and fusible appliqué and are so fun to assemble.

Finished Door Banner: 17½" x 42¼"
Pieced and appliquéd by Cheryl Almgren Taylor; quilted by Cheryl Winslow.

MATERIALS
Yardage is based on 42"-wide fabric.

⅔ yard of black fabric for inner border and bias binding

½ yard *total* of 2 different sky blue fabrics for Winter Scene and Welcome block backgrounds

½ yard of tan fabric for Holly block backgrounds

½ yard of red print for outer border and appliqués

¼ yard of white-on-white print for Winter Scene blocks and appliqués

¼ yard *total* of assorted green prints for appliqués

Scraps of assorted brown, red, orange, cream, tan, white, gold, and gray prints for appliqués

1⅜ yards of fabric for backing

21" x 46" piece of batting

1¼ yards of 22"-wide lightweight paper-backed fusible web

Assorted matching threads for appliqué

Black fine-point permanent marker

CUTTING

From the 2 sky blue fabrics, cut a *total* of:
- 3 rectangles, 9" x 14"
- 1 rectangle, 3½" x 14"

From the white-on-white print, cut:
- 3 rectangles, 2" x 14"

From the tan fabric, cut:
- 5 rectangles, 3¼" x 14"

From the black fabric, cut:
- 3 strips, 1" x 42"
- Enough 2½"-wide bias strips to make a 130" length of binding when pieced together

From the red print, cut:
- 3 strips, 2" x 42"

Welcome and Holly blocks

Winter Scene 1

Winter Scene 2

Winter Scene 3

Making the Blocks

1. Refer to "Fusible-Web Appliqué" on page 11 to prepare the appliqué pieces on pages 25–29 for use. Consult the materials list and the photo on page 20 for fabric choices if needed. Preassemble some of the shapes if desired. Use the marker to draw in the snowman's eyes, mouth, and buttons.

2. Sew a white 2" x 14" rectangle to the bottom of each blue 9" x 14" rectangle. Press the seam allowances toward the blue rectangles. These will be the backgrounds for Winter Scenes 1–3.

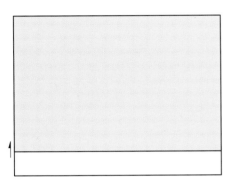

3. Using the placement guides at right for reference and referring to the numbers on the patterns, position the Winter Scene 1–3 appliqués on the step 2 background pieces, the "WELCOME" letters on the blue 3½" x 14" rectangle, and the holly and berry appliqués on the tan rectangles in numerical order. The background blocks are slightly oversized to allow for the shrinkage that usually occurs with appliqué; you will trim them to size after all the shapes have been adhered. Keep the following in mind when positioning the appliqués:

   Winter Scene blocks: The *finished* blocks will measure 8" x 13". Place the bottom of the houses on the seam line between the blue and white fabrics.

   Welcome block: The *finished* block will measure 2½" x 13". Center the letters within this space.

   Holly blocks: The *finished* blocks will measure 2¼" x 13". Center the design within this space.

   Work on one block at a time. After all the pieces for that block have been positioned, fuse the pieces in place, following the manufacturer's instructions.

4. Finish the raw edges of each appliqué piece using a blanket stitch, zigzag stitch, or satin stitch.

Winter Scene 1 placement guide

Winter Scene 2 placement guide

Winter Scene 3 placement guide

Holly block placement guide

5. Use a narrow zigzag stitch to create the flame for each candle in Winter Scene 2. You may want to experiment on some fabric scraps before stitching on the block.

6. Square up the blocks to the following sizes, keeping the designs centered:

   Winter Scene blocks: 8½" x 13½"

   Welcome block: 3" x 13½"

   Holly blocks: 2¾" x 13½"

ASSEMBLING THE BANNER

1. Sew Holly blocks to the top and bottom edges of the Welcome block, and to the bottom of each Winter Scene block. Press the seam allowances toward the Holly blocks.

2. Refer to the assembly diagram to sew the blocks together in the order shown. Press the seam allowances toward the Holly blocks.

3. Refer to "Adding Borders" on page 14 to measure the quilt top for the borders. Add the black 1"-wide inner border first, and then add the red 2"-wide outer border using the butted-corners method.

FINISHING THE BANNER

1. Prepare the backing so that it is 4" longer and 4" wider than the banner top.

2. Layer the backing, batting, and quilt top, and baste together.

3. Quilt as desired.

4. When the quilting is complete, square up the banner sandwich. Refer to "Binding" on page 16 to attach the bias binding.

5. Add a hanging sleeve and a label to the back of your banner.

Quilt assembly

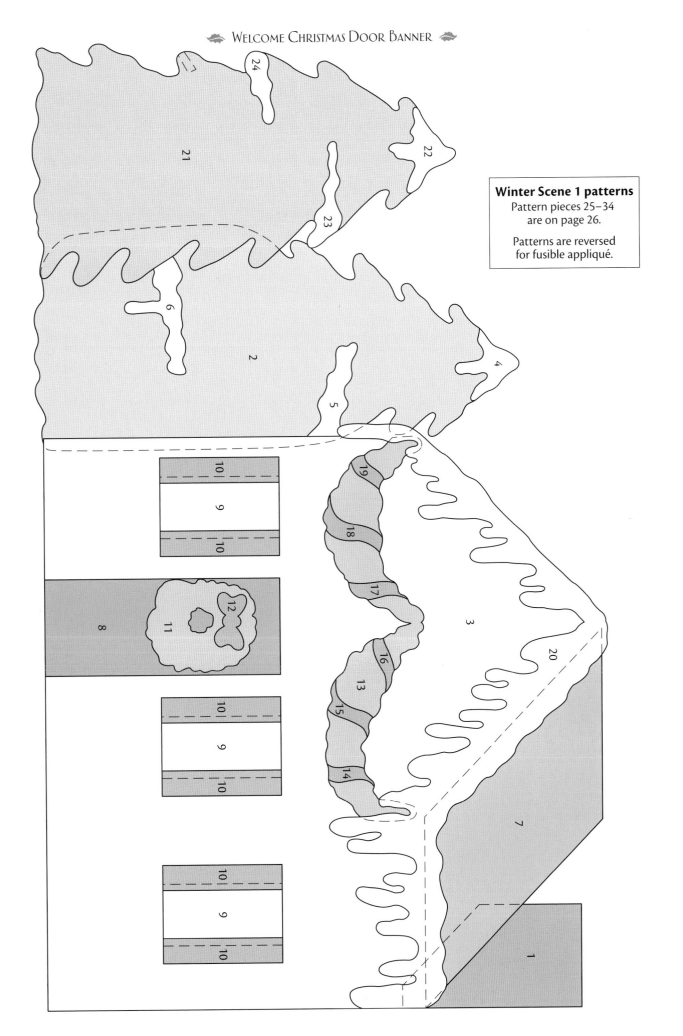

Winter Scene 1 patterns
Pattern pieces 25–34
are on page 26.

Patterns are reversed
for fusible appliqué.

26

27

25

28

33

34

32

Draw details.

29

30

31

21

16

22

23

24

25

26

Winter Scene 1 patterns
Patterns are reversed
for fusible appliqué.

Winter Scene 2 patterns
Patterns are reversed
for fusible appliqué.

Winter Scene 2 patterns
Patterns are reversed
for fusible appliqué.

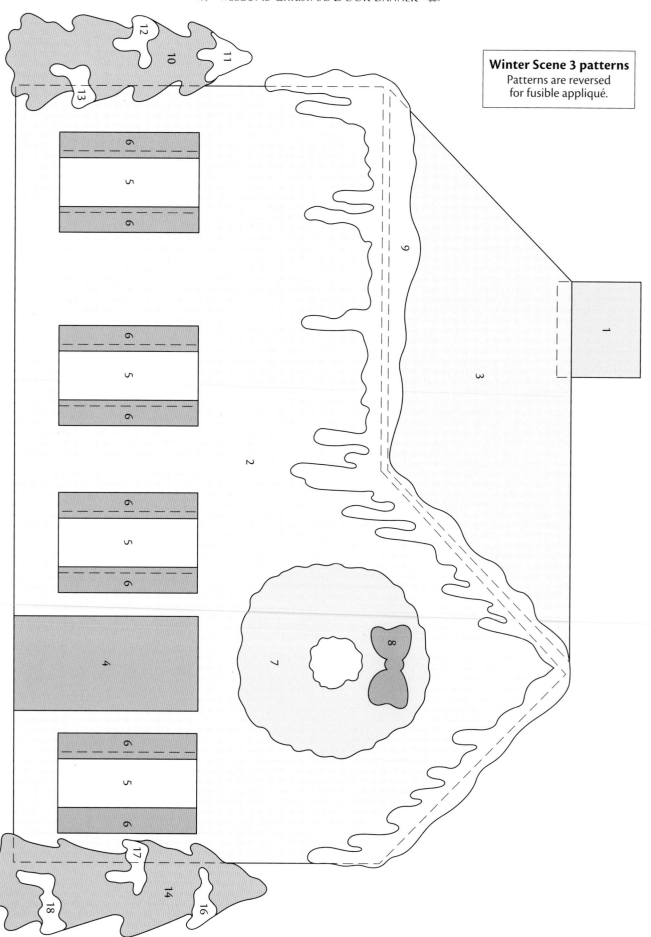

Winter Scene 3 patterns
Patterns are reversed
for fusible appliqué.

19

20

15

21

W
E
L
C
O
M
E

Winter Scene 3 patterns
Patterns are reversed
for fusible appliqué.

Welcome block patterns
Make 2 of E and 1 each
of remaining letters.
Patterns are reversed
for fusible appliqué.

1
Make 60.

2
Make 75.

Holly block patterns
Patterns are reversed
for fusible appliqué.

PRETTY POINSETTIAS QUILT

This pretty quilt is created with simple piecing and fast, fusible appliqué. The use of a variety of red fabrics, including some with gold metallic designs, adds interest to the poinsettia appliqués. The flowers are quilted with gold metallic thread, adding even more glitz. Gold beads stitched to the center of each flower give the quilt an extra dimension of texture and elegance.

MATERIALS

Yardage is based on 42"-wide fabric.

⅞ yard of white print for block backgrounds

⅞ yard of red-and-gold dot print for inner border and bias binding

⅝ yard of holly print for outer border

⅜ yard of green-and-white dot print for sashing

⅜ yard *total* of 4 assorted red prints that read as solid for poinsettia appliqués

⅜ yard *total* of 4 assorted red-and-gold metallic prints for poinsettia appliqués

¼ yard *total* of 2 different green prints for poinsettia leaf appliqués

⅛ yard of red print with gold motif for sashing squares

1¼ yards of fabric for backing

41½" x 41½" square of batting

¾ yard of 22"-wide lightweight paper-backed fusible web

54 gold metallic beads, 4 mm

Gold metallic thread for quilting

CUTTING

From the white print, cut:

• 9 squares, 9" x 9"

From the green-and-white dot print, cut:

• 24 rectangles, 1¾" x 8½"

From the red print with gold motif, cut:

• 16 squares, 1¾" x 1¾", centering a motif in each square

From the red-and-gold dot print, cut:

• 4 strips, 1¼" x 42"

• Enough 2½"-wide bias strips to make a 160" length of binding when pieced together

From the holly print, cut:

• 4 strips, 3¾" x 42"

Finished Quilt: 37½" x 37½"
Finished Block: 8" x 8"
Pieced and quilted by Cheryl Almgren Taylor.

Making the Appliqué Blocks

1. Refer to "Fusible-Web Appliqué" on page 11 to prepare the appliqué pieces on page 35 from the fabrics indicated. You might want to plan ahead and decide which two red fabrics you will use in each block. I like to use a red fabric and a red-and-gold fabric in each block for a scrappy look, alternating where I use the red-and-gold fabric (either in the upper or lower bracts). Do the same for the green leaf prints if desired.

2. Select the pieces for each block if you have not already determined this. Referring to the placement guide, center and arrange the pieces for one block on a white print square in the order indicated. Follow the manufacturer's instructions to fuse the shapes in place. Repeat to make a total of nine blocks.

Placement guide

3. Finish the raw edges of each appliqué piece using a blanket stitch, zigzag stitch, or satin stitch.

4. Square up the completed blocks to 8½" x 8½", keeping the designs centered.

Assembling the Quilt Top

1. Alternately join four green-and-white 1¾" x 8½" sashing strips and three blocks to make a block row. Repeat to make a total of three rows. Press the seam allowances toward the sashing strips.

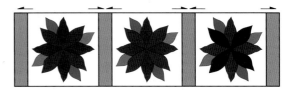

Make 3.

2. To make the sashing rows, alternately join four gold-motif 1¾" squares and three green-and-white 1¾" x 8½" sashing strips. Repeat to make a total of four rows. Press the seam allowances toward the sashing strips.

Make 4.

3. Refer to the quilt assembly diagram to alternately sew the sashing and block rows together. Press the seam allowances toward the sashing rows. The quilt top should measure 29" x 29".

4. Refer to "Adding Borders" on page 14 to measure the quilt top for the borders. Add the red-and-gold 1¼"-wide inner border first, and then add the holly print 3¾"-wide outer border, using the butted-corners method.

FINISHING THE QUILT

1. Prepare the backing so that it is 4" longer and 4" wider than the quilt top.

2. Layer the backing, batting, and quilt top, and baste together.

3. Quilt as desired. I recommend using some metallic thread to add Christmas sparkle to the quilt.

4. When the quilting is complete, square up the quilt sandwich. Refer to "Binding" on page 16 to attach the bias binding.

5. Hand stitch six gold beads to the center of each flower. When attaching the beads, go into the batting but not all the way through the backing fabric. This will firmly attach the beads but keep the back of your quilt looking nice.

6. Add a hanging sleeve and a label to your quilt.

Quilt assembly

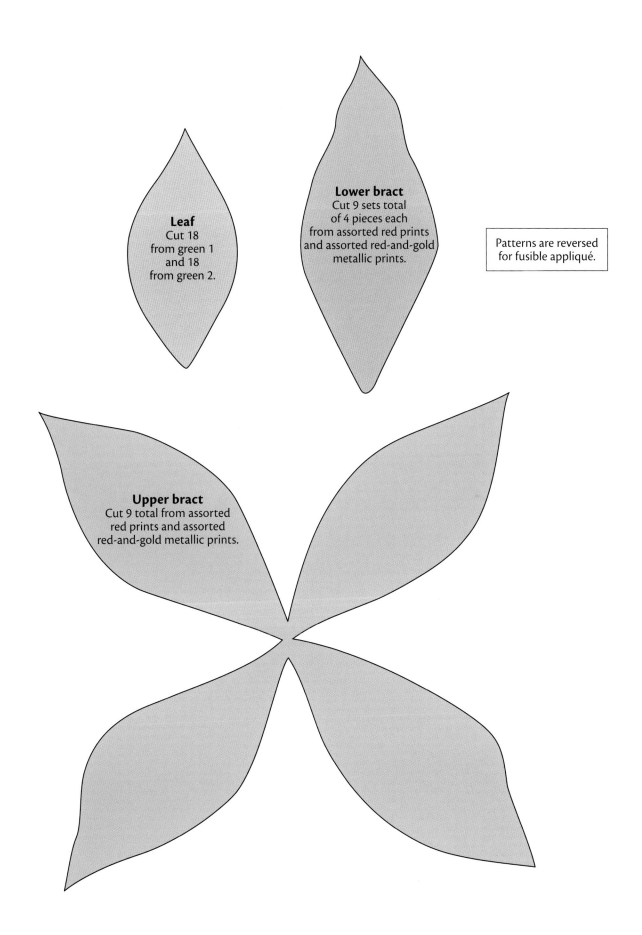

Leaf
Cut 18
from green 1
and 18
from green 2.

Lower bract
Cut 9 sets total
of 4 pieces each
from assorted red prints
and assorted red-and-gold
metallic prints.

Patterns are reversed
for fusible appliqué.

Upper bract
Cut 9 total from assorted
red prints and assorted
red-and-gold metallic prints.

YULETIDE ORNAMENTS MANTEL RUNNER

Decorate your fireplace with this festive garland that has just a touch of radiant sparkle.
Thanks to fusible-web appliqué and paper piecing, the design is easy to sew. What a
beautiful accessory to warm your home as you cuddle by the hearth!

MATERIALS

Yardage is based on 42"-wide fabric.

1¾ yards of red print for background and bias binding

½ yard *total* of assorted green batiks for bias vines and leaf appliqués

⅛ yard of gold print for ornament appliqués

Scraps of red, white, and black fabrics with metallic print for ornament appliqués

1⅓ yards of fabric for backing

20" x 60" piece of batting

½ yard of ⅛"-wide gold metallic ribbon for ornament hanger appliqués

Tracing paper

¾ yard of 22"-wide lightweight paper-backed fusible web

Assorted matching threads for appliqué

Foundation paper for paper piecing

White chalk marking pencil

CUTTING

From the red print, cut:

- 2 strips, 7" x 42"
- 2 strips, 10¼" x 42"
- Enough 2½"-wide bias strips to make a 155" length of binding when pieced together

From the assorted green batiks, cut a *total* of:

- 5 bias strips, 1¼" x 13"

PREPARING THE APPLIQUÉ SECTION BACKGROUND

1. Trace the scallop pattern on pages 42 and 43 onto tracing paper and cut it out.

2. Sew the ends of the 7" x 42" strips together to make one long strip. Press the seam allowance open. Align the center mark on the pattern with the seam line. Using the chalk pencil, trace the curved edge of the pattern onto the fabric. Reposition the template to the right of the completed tracing, aligning the ends, and trace another section. Repeat once more to the right and then trace two sections to the left of the center mark for a total of five sections. Measure ¼" from the ends of the first and last template markings and draw a line. Cut on the end lines to remove the excess fabric. *Do not cut along the scalloped edge.*

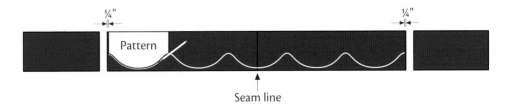

Finished Mantel Runner: 55½" x 16¾"

Pieced and quilted by Cheryl Almgren Taylor.

3. Use the template and the chalk pencil to mark the position of the vines on the right side of the strip in each of the five sections.

MAKING THE ORNAMENT APPLIQUÉS

1. Referring to "Paper Piecing" on page 13, make 15 copies of the paper-piecing pattern on page 41. Using the assorted scraps of metallic fabrics, paper piece the foundations. Use the black scrap for area 1 on nine of the foundations, the red scrap for area 1 on the remaining six foundations, and the white scrap for areas 2–5 on all the foundations.

2. Sew three matching units together side by side. Repeat to make a total of five ornament center units.

3. Using the pattern on page 41, trace 10 ornament halves onto the paper side of the fusible web, leaving at least ½" between the shapes. Cut away the center portion. Fuse the web to the back of the gold metallic fabric. Cut out the halves, *leaving a ¼" seam allowance on the straight edge.* Do not remove the paper backing.

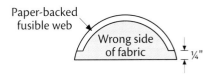

4. Center and sew an ornament half to each long side of the paper-pieced units. Remove the paper foundation from the pieced units, but *do not* remove the paper backing from the fusible web. Press the seam allowances toward the gold fabric. Round out the sides of the pieced center units to create a circle shape.

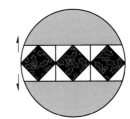

Make 5.

DESIGN ADJUSTMENTS

This swag is designed for a mantel that is 55½" long and 10" deep, but the dimensions can be adjusted to fit your own space. Begin by measuring your mantel length and depth. For example, let's say your mantel is 72" long and 8" deep.

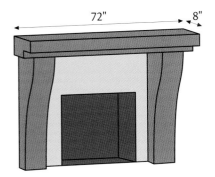

The garland-and-ornament design repeats every 11". Divide the length of your mantel by 11 to see how many garland repeats you will need. In our example, you could use 6 garland repeats (6 x 11" = 66") and the swag would end 3" from each end of the mantel. If you prefer to have the swag extend past the mantel, you could use 7 repeats (7 x 11" = 77") and the swag would hang off the mantel edge 2½" on each side.

OR

To adjust the top section of the mantel swag, add ¼" seam allowance to the depth measured and cut the piece that width (8" + ¼" = 8¼") by the length you selected.

APPLIQUÉING THE DESIGN

1. Fold each green batik bias strip in half lengthwise, wrong sides together. Refer to steps 3–5 of "Making and Appliquéing Bias Vines" on page 12 to make the vines and stitch them to the previously marked lines on the appliqué section background. Make sure the vines extend into the seam allowance.

2. Cut the ribbon into five 2½" lengths for the ornament hangers. Refer to the placement guide on page 41 to position the pieces on the background strip in each of the five sections. One end of the ribbon should extend into the seam allowance and over the ends of the vines at the top of the strip. Sew along both long edges of the ribbon.

3. Refer to "Fusible-Web Appliqué" on page 11 and use the patterns on page 41 to prepare the ornament topper and leaf appliqués from the fabrics indicated. Refer to the placement guide to arrange the pieces on each section in the order indicated. Follow the manufacturer's instructions to fuse the shapes in place.

4. Finish the raw edges of each appliqué piece, except for the ornament hanger, using a blanket stitch, zig-zag stitch, or satin stitch.

5. Create the scalloped edge by trimming away the excess fabric along the marked line at the bottom of the appliquéd section.

ASSEMBLING THE MANTEL RUNNER

1. Sew the ends of the red 10¼" x 42" strips together to make one long strip. Press the seam allowance open. Trim the strip to 55½", keeping the seam line centered. To do this, measure 27¾" from each side of the seam line and trim away the excess fabric.

2. Sew the mantel top section to the appliquéd section, matching the seam lines. Press the seam allowance toward the appliquéd section.

FINISHING THE MANTEL RUNNER

1. Prepare the backing so that it is 4" longer and 4" wider than the runner top. *Do not cut the scallops in the backing fabric.*

2. Layer the backing, batting, and runner top, and baste together.

3. Quilt as desired. I recommend using some metallic thread to add Christmas sparkle to the quilt.

4. When the quilting is complete, square up the back and sides of the runner sandwich. Trim the batting and backing even with the scalloped edge. Refer to "Binding" on page 16 to attach the bias binding.

5. Add a label to the back of your runner.

Placement guide

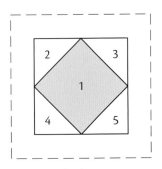

Paper-piecing pattern

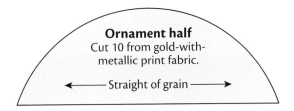

Ornament half
Cut 10 from gold-with-metallic print fabric.

←——— Straight of grain ———→

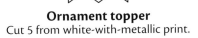

Ornament topper
Cut 5 from white-with-metallic print.

Leaf
Cut 80 from assorted green batiks.

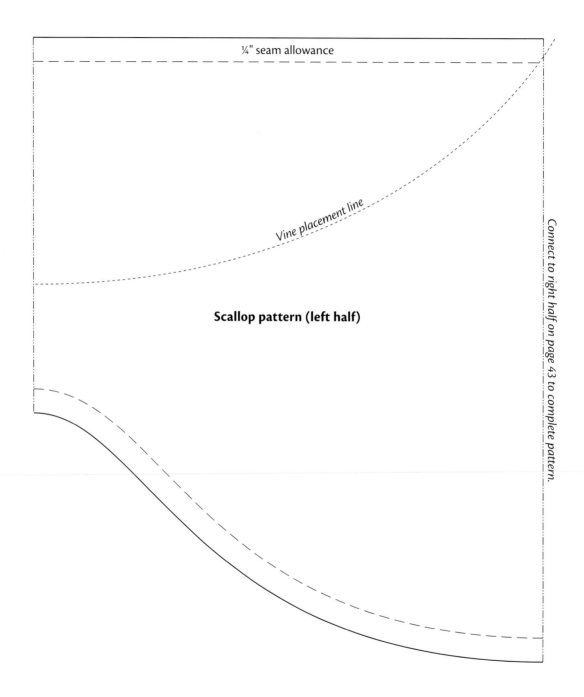

¼" seam allowance

Vine placement line

Scallop pattern (left half)

Connect to right half on page 43 to complete pattern.

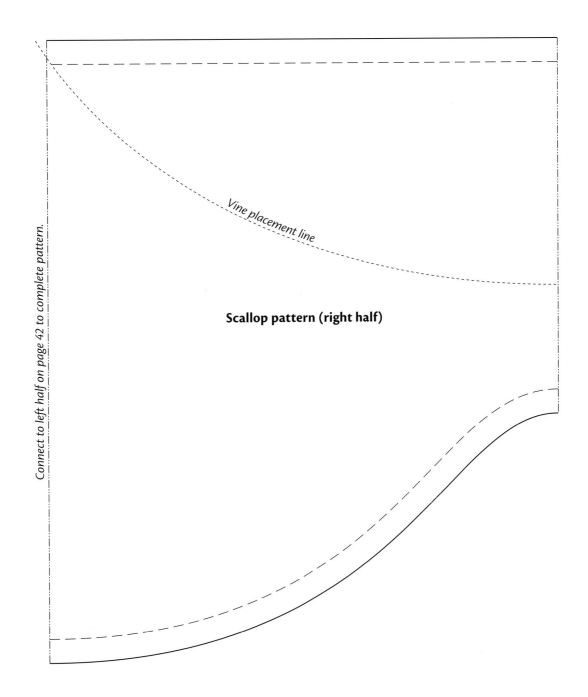

Connect to left half on page 42 to complete pattern.

Vine placement line

Scallop pattern (right half)

POMEGRANATES AND POSIES QUILT

This traditional quilt features pomegranates and roses in rich red tones for holiday opulence. Shades of cream and gold provide a warm background to the flowing vines, creating an elegant addition to your Christmas decor.

MATERIALS

Yardage is based on 42"-wide fabric.

2 yards of light gold fabric for center block and outer border

1 yard *total* of assorted green batiks for vines and leaf appliqués

⅞ yard of cream fabric for dogtooth border and quilt center setting triangles

⅞ yard of deep red fabric for inner border and bias binding

⅔ yard *total* of 6 assorted red fabrics for dogtooth border and pomegranate and posy appliqués

Scraps of assorted pink, rose, and purple batiks for pomegranate and posy appliqués

3¼ yards of fabric for backing

52" x 52" square of batting

1½ yards of 22"-wide lightweight paper-backed fusible web

Assorted matching threads and gold metallic thread for appliqué

CUTTING

From the light gold fabric, cut:

- 1 square, 21" x 21"
- 6 strips, 6¾" x 42"

From the 6 assorted red fabrics, cut a *total* of:

- 6 strips, 2½" x 19"

From the cream fabric, cut:

- 2 squares, 16⅞" x 16⅞"; cut once diagonally to yield 4 half-square triangles
- 3 strips, 2½" x 42"; crosscut into 6 strips, 2½" x 19"
- 4 squares, 1¾" x 1¾"

From the deep red fabric, cut:

- 4 strips, 1¾" x 42"
- Enough 2½"-wide bias strips to make a 200" length of binding when pieced together

Finished Quilt: 47½" x 47½"
Pieced by Cheryl Almgren Taylor; quilted by Cheryl Winslow.

PREPARING THE APPLIQUÉS

1. Referring to "Making and Appliquéing Bias Vines" on page 12, cut 1¼"-wide bias strips and make ¼"-wide finished stems in the following lengths and amounts:

   4 stems each: 24", 8", 6½", 4"

   8 stems each: 11½", 11", 6¼", 2½"

2. Refer to "Fusible-Web Appliqué" on page 11 and use the patterns on pages 50 and 51 to prepare the pomegranate, posy, and leaf appliqués from the fabrics indicated.

APPLIQUÉING THE QUILT CENTER PIECES

1. Refer to the center block placement guide and "Making and Appliquéing Bias Vines" to appliqué vines of the appropriate length to the gold square. Refer to the corner placement guide to appliqué the appropriate vines to the cream half-square triangles. Set aside the remaining vines for the outer border.

2. Refer to the center block placement guide and the corner placement guide to arrange the prepared appliqué pieces on the gold square and the cream triangles in the order indicated. Be sure to position pieces over the ends of the vines. Follow the manufacturer's instructions to fuse the shapes in place.

3. Finish the raw edges of each appliqué piece using a blanket stitch, zigzag stitch, or satin stitch. I recommend using gold metallic thread on the pomegranates to give them a nice sparkle.

4. Square up the center block to 20½" x 20½".

MAKING THE DOGTOOTH BORDER

1. Sew each assorted red 2½" x 19" strip to a cream 2½" x 19" strip to make a strip set. Press the seam allowances toward the red strips. Draw a line on the wrong side of the red strips, ½" from the long edges. Crosscut the strip sets into 40 segments, 2¼" wide.

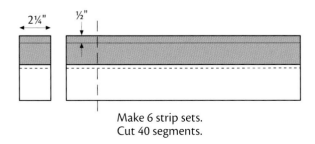

Make 6 strip sets.
Cut 40 segments.

2. Join 10 segments, staggering the pieces so that the *drawn line* on one segment matches the *seam line* of the adjacent segment. Repeat to make a total of four border units. Press the seam allowances in one direction. Be careful not to stretch the units.

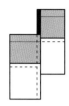

3. With the red segments on top and the white segments on the bottom, lay your ruler across the red segments and mark ¼" above the point of the cream triangles. Next, lay your ruler on the cream segments and mark another line ¼" from the point of the red triangles. Cut along these lines. Repeat for the remaining border units.

4. Trim the ends of each border unit ¼" from the seam line joining the red and cream strips.

ASSEMBLING THE QUILT TOP

1. Refer to the quilt assembly diagram to stitch dogtooth border units to opposite sides of the center block, positioning the red triangles closest to the block. Press the seam allowances toward the borders. Sew a cream 1¾" square to each end of the remaining two border units, and then sew these strips to the remaining sides of the center block in the same manner; press. The quilt top should measure 23" square.

2. Sew appliquéd corner triangles to opposite sides of the quilt top. Press the seam allowances toward the triangles. Repeat on the remaining two sides; press. The quilt top should now measure 32½" square.

3. Refer to "Adding Borders" on page 14 to measure the quilt top for borders. Add the deep red 1¾"-wide border using the butted-corners method, and then add the gold 6¾"-wide outer border using the mitered-corners method.

4. Refer to the outer border placement guide and "Making and Appliquéing Bias Vines" to appliqué vines of the appropriate length to each corner of the outer border. Arrange the remaining appliqué pieces on each corner in the order indicated. Be sure to position pieces over the ends of the vines. Follow the manufacturer's instructions to fuse the shapes in place. Finish the raw edges of each appliqué piece using a blanket stitch, zigzag stitch, or satin stitch. Again, I recommend using gold metallic thread on the pomegranates. Trim the borders as necessary to allow for any distortion that may have occurred during the appliqué process.

APPLIQUÉING ON LARGE PIECES

To more easily finish the raw appliqué edges when dealing with a large piece of fabric, fold up the parts of the quilt that you are not working on. Unfold and refold as needed while doing your stitching. This will also help minimize fraying along the raw edges.

FINISHING THE QUILT

1. Prepare the backing so that it is 4" longer and 4" wider than the quilt top.

2. Layer the backing, batting, and quilt top, and baste together.

3. Quilt as desired.

4. When the quilting is complete, square up the quilt sandwich. Refer to "Binding" on page 16 to attach the binding.

5. Add a hanging sleeve and a label to the back of your quilt.

Quilt assembly

Center block placement guide
A: 8" stem
B: 6½" stem
C: 4" stem

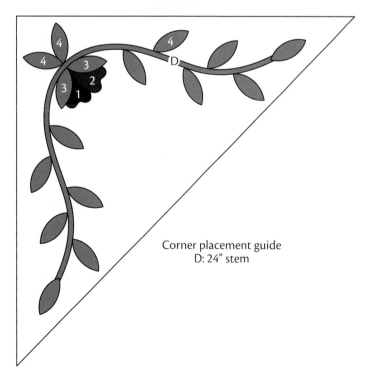

Corner placement guide
D: 24" stem

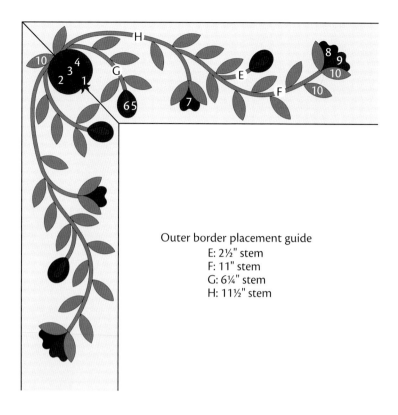

Outer border placement guide
E: 2½" stem
F: 11" stem
G: 6¼" stem
H: 11½" stem

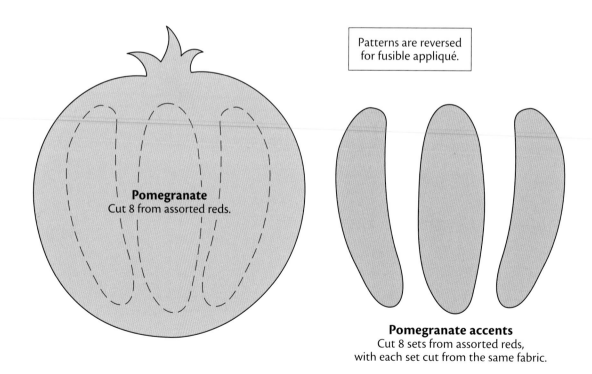

Pomegranate
Cut 8 from assorted reds.

Patterns are reversed
for fusible appliqué.

Pomegranate accents
Cut 8 sets from assorted reds,
with each set cut from the same fabric.

Patterns are reversed
for fusible appliqué.

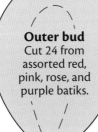

Outer bud
Cut 24 from
assorted red,
pink, rose, and
purple batiks.

Inner bud
Cut 24 from
assorted red,
pink, rose, and
purple batiks.

Quilt center large posy petal
Cut 6 from assorted reds.

**Quilt center
small posy petal**
Cut 3 from assorted reds.

Vine petal
Cut 32 from
assorted red,
pink, rose, and
purple batiks.

Leaf
Cut 268 from
assorted
green batiks.

TERRIFIC TABLETOPS

A wonderful way to make your house feel festive for the holidays is by decorating the dining-room table with some Christmas style. Sew up one of the quick-and-easy table quilts featured in this section and display it throughout the season. Keep the table set with holiday dishes and stemware to add even more warmth and elegance to your home.

PEPPERMINT CANDY TABLE RUNNER

This bright, cheerful table runner features pieced Pinwheel blocks that look like peppermint candies. Using different red and green fabrics gives each block its own personality and helps use up some of your stash. This runner is so easy that you may just want to make several to have on hand for last-minute gifts.

MATERIALS

Yardage is based on 42"-wide fabric.

⅔ yard of green print for middle border and bias binding

⅝ yard of white print for blocks and pieced inner and outer borders

⅓ yard of red dot print for blocks and pieced inner and outer borders

¼ yard *total* of assorted green prints for blocks

¼ yard *total* of assorted red prints for blocks

⅝ yard of fabric for backing

16" x 40" piece of batting

CUTTING

From the white print, cut:

- 10 squares, 3" x 3"
- 4 strips, 2½" x 21"; crosscut 1 strip into 8 squares, 1½" x 1½"

From the assorted red prints, cut a *total* of:

- 9 squares, 3" x 3"

From the assorted green prints, cut a *total* of:

- 5 pairs of squares, 3⅞" x 3⅞"; cut once diagonally to yield 20 half-square triangles

From the red dot print, cut:

- 1 square, 3" x 3"
- 4 strips, 2½" x 21"; crosscut 1 strip into 8 rectangles, 1½" x 2"

From the green print for middle border and binding, cut:

- 3 strips, 1" x 42"; crosscut into:
  - 2 strips, 1" x 32½"
  - 2 strips, 1" x 9½"
- Enough 2½"-wide bias strips to make a 104" length of binding when pieced together

Finished Table Runner: 11½" x 35½"
Finished Block: 6" x 6"

Pieced by Cheryl Almgren Taylor;
machine quilted by Cheryl Winslow.

Making the Blocks

1. Place a white 3" square on top of each assorted red and red dot 3" square, right sides together. Using a pencil and ruler, draw a diagonal line from corner to corner on the wrong side of the white squares. Sew ¼" from both sides of the marked line. Cut the squares apart on the drawn line and press the seam allowances toward the red. Each pair of squares will make two half-square-triangle units.

Make 20.

2. Sew two different half-square-triangle units together as shown. Repeat to make a total of 10 pairs. Sew 2 pairs together to make a block center. Repeat to make a total of five block centers.

Make 5.

3. Sew four matching green triangles to the sides of each block center, adding opposite sides first. Press the seam allowances toward the triangles. The blocks should measure 6½" x 6½".

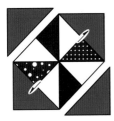 

Make 5.

Assembling the Table Runner Top

1. Sew the blocks together side by side. Press the seam allowances toward the second and fourth blocks. The runner top must measure 6½" x 30½" or the pieced borders will not fit.

2. To make the pieced inner border, sew a red dot 2½" x 21" strip to each long side of a white 2½" x 21" strip to make strip set A. Sew a white 2½" x 21" strip to each long side of a red dot 2½" x 21" strip to make strip set B. Press the seam allowances toward the red. Crosscut each strip set into 12 segments, 1½" wide.

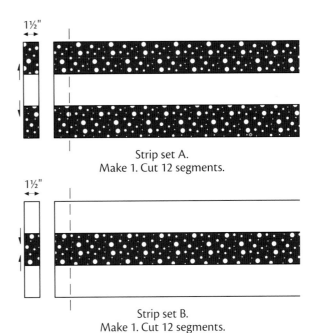

1½"

Strip set A.
Make 1. Cut 12 segments.

1½"

Strip set B.
Make 1. Cut 12 segments.

3. Alternately sew three A segments and two B segments together end to end. Press the seam allowances toward the A segments. Repeat to make a total of two strips. Sew the strips to the long edges of the runner top. Press the seam allowances toward the borders. Sew a white 1½" square to each end of two A segments. Press the seam allowances toward the A segments. Add these border strips to the short edges of the runner top. Press the seam allowances toward the borders.

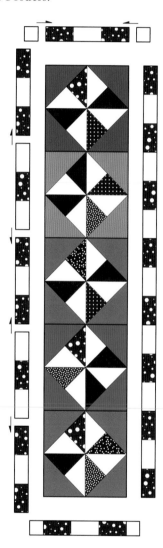

5. Alternately sew three B segments and two A segments together end to end. Add a red dot 1½" x 2" rectangle to each end of the strip. Press the seam allowances toward the A segments and the red dot rectangles. Repeat to make a total of two strips. Sew these strips to the long edges of the runner top. Press the seam allowances toward the green border. Sew a red dot 1½" x 2" rectangle and then a white 1½" square to each end of the remaining two B segments. Press the seam allowances toward the red rectangles. Add these strips to the short edges of the table runner top. Press the seam allowances toward the green border.

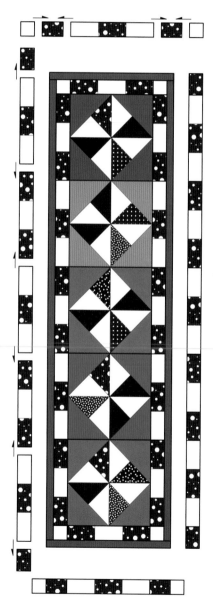

4. Sew the green 1" x 32½" strips to the long edges of the runner top. Press the seam allowances toward the green borders. Sew the green 1" x 9½" strips to the short edges of the runner top. Press the seam allowances toward the green borders. The runner top must now measure 9½" x 33½" or the pieced outer border will not fit.

Finishing the Table Runner

1. Trim the backing fabric so that it is 4" longer and 4" wider than the table runner top.

2. Layer the backing, batting, and runner top, and baste together.

3. Quilt as desired. The table runner shown in the project photo on page 54 was quilted with gold metallic thread.

4. When the quilting is complete, square up the table runner sandwich. Refer to "Binding" on page 16 to attach the bias binding.

5. Add a label to the back of your runner.

PERFECT PRESENTS

For quick and easy Christmas presents, use the versatile Pinwheel block to create decorative pillows. Four blocks, arranged as shown, will make a 12" pillow. If you would like a larger pillow, add border strips to the sides. Remember to add ½" to the desired finished width of the border strips for seam allowances and to adjust the size of the backing pieces.

1. To make the pillow top, refer to the table runner instructions to make four blocks. Sew the blocks into two rows of two blocks each, and then sew the rows together.

2. To make the pillow back, cut two rectangles, 8" x 12½". On each rectangle, press under one long edge ¼" twice and stitch down the hem.

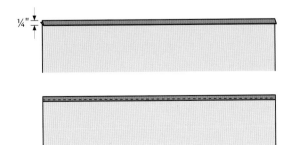

3. With right sides facing up, overlap the hemmed edges of the rectangles to create a 12½" square. Baste the side edges together at the overlap.

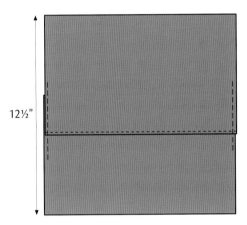

12½"

4. Position the pillow front over the backing pieces, right sides together. Stitch around the pillow cover using a ¼" seam allowance.

5. Turn the pillow cover to the right side and insert a 12" pillow form through the opening in the back.

HOLLY BERRY TABLE TOPPER

This small quilt is sure to brighten a holiday meal, whether it's topping a table or gracing the wall as a festive decoration. This is an easy design for beginning quilters because of the large, simple appliqué pieces.

MATERIALS

Yardage is based on 42"-wide fabric.

1⅜ yards of red print for blocks, outer border, and bias binding

1⅛ yards of cream print for blocks and inner border

⅓ yard of dark green print 1 for sashing

¼ yard of gold print for sashing

¼ yard of dark green print 2 for holly appliqués

Scraps of assorted red fabrics for berry appliqués

2⅞ yards of fabric for backing

47" x 47" square of batting

Assorted matching threads for appliqué

CUTTING

From the cream print, cut:

- 4 squares, 9" x 9"
- 4 strips, 6½" x 42"

From the red print, cut:

- 8 squares, 6½" x 6½"; cut once diagonally to yield 16 triangles
- 5 strips, 2" x 42"
- Enough 2½"-wide bias strips to make a 180" length of binding when pieced together

From the dark green print 1, cut:

- 9 strips, 1" x 42"; cut 1 strip in half crosswise to yield 2 strips, 1" x 21" (you will have 1 left over)

From the gold print, cut:

- 5 strips, 1" x 42"; cut *1* strip in half crosswise to yield 2 strips, 1" x 21"

MAKING THE BLOCKS

1. Refer to "Fusible-Web Appliqué" on page 11 and use the patterns on pages 65 to prepare the holly and berry appliqués from the fabrics indicated.

2. Refer to the block placement guide to arrange the prepared appliqué pieces on the cream print squares in the order indicated. Follow the manufacturer's instructions to fuse the shapes in place.

Block placement guide

Finished Table Topper: 42½" x 42½"
Finished Block: 11¼" x 11¼"
Pieced and quilted by Debbie Lindgren.

3. Finish the raw edges of each appliqué piece using a blanket stitch, zigzag stitch, or satin stitch.

4. Square up each square to 8½" x 8½".

5. Sew a red triangle to each side of the appliquéd squares, adding opposite sides first. Press the seam allowances toward the triangles. Square up the blocks to 11¾" square.

Make 4.

MAKING THE SASHING PIECES

1. Sew a dark green 1" x 42" strip to each long edge of a gold 1" x 42" strip to make strip set A. Repeat to make a total of four strip sets. Press the seam allowances toward the green strips. Crosscut the strip sets into 12 segments, 11¾" wide, and 9 segments, 1" wide.

Strip set A.
Make 4. Cut 12 segments, 11¾" wide,
and 9 segments, 1" wide.

2. Sew a gold 1" x 21" strip to each long edge of a dark green 1" x 21" strip to make strip set B. Press the seam allowances toward the green strip. Crosscut the strip set into 18 segments, 1" wide.

Strip set B.
Make 1. Cut 18 segments.

3. Join B segments to the sides of each 1"-wide A segment to make a nine-patch unit. Make a total of nine units.

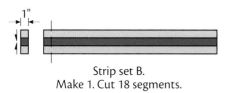

Make 9.

ASSEMBLING THE TABLE TOPPER

1. Alternately join three 11¾" strip set A sashing segments and two blocks to make a block row. Press the seam allowances toward the sashing. Repeat to make a total of two rows.

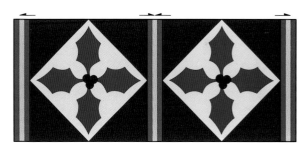

Make 2.

2. Alternately join three nine-patch units and two sashing segments to make a sashing row. Press the seam allowances toward the sashing. Repeat to make a total of three rows.

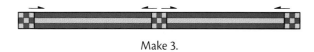

Make 3.

3. Refer to the quilt assembly diagram to alternately sew the sashing rows and block rows together. Press the seam allowances toward the sashing rows.

4. Refer to "Adding Borders" on page 14 to measure the table topper for the borders. Add the cream 6½"-wide inner border using the butted-corners method.

5. Refer to the corner and side placement guides on page 65 to arrange the remaining prepared appliqué pieces on the border in the order indicated. Follow the manufacturer's instructions to fuse the shapes in place. Finish the raw edges of each appliqué piece using a blanket stitch, zigzag stitch, or satin stitch.

6. Join the red 2"-wide outer border to the quilt top using the butted-corners method.

FINISHING THE TABLE TOPPER

1. Trim the backing fabric so that it is 4" longer and 4" wider than the quilt top.

2. Layer the backing, batting, and quilt top, and baste together.

3. Quilt as desired.

4. When the quilting is complete, square up the table topper sandwich. Refer to "Binding" on page 16 to attach bias binding.

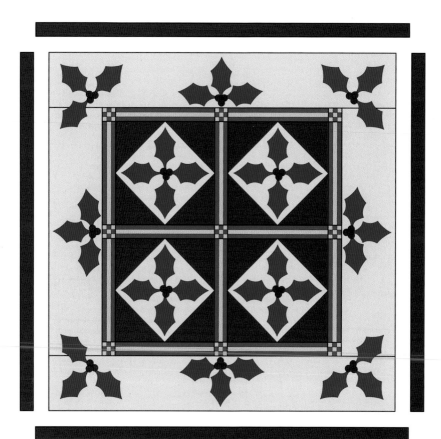

Quilt assembly

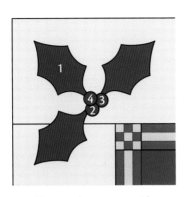

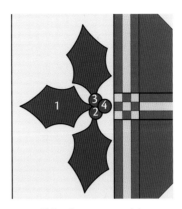

Corner placement guide   Side placement guide

Leaf
Cut 40 from dark green 2.

Berry
Cut 36 from
assorted
reds.

WRAPPED UP IN RIBBONS TABLE RUNNER

This whimsical table runner sets the mood for a merry Christmas. The center section is made from three easy blocks, adorned with just a little appliqué. The zigzag border adds some pizzazz and is made from simple flying-geese units. It's easy enough for a confident beginner and would make a great last-minute gift.

MATERIALS

Yardage is based on 42"-wide fabric.

⅞ yard of red-on-red polka-dot fabric for ribbon appliqués, flying-geese units, and bias binding

⅓ yard of holly print for block backgrounds and third border

⅓ yard of cream print for sashing, first border, and flying-geese units

⅓ yard of green checked fabric for ribbon appliqués and flying-geese units

¼ yard of candy cane print for block background

⅛ yard of red print for blocks and ribbon appliqués

⅛ yard of green print for blocks and ribbon appliqués

⅔ yard of fabric for backing

20" x 38" piece of batting

½ yard of 22"-wide lightweight paper-backed fusible web

CUTTING

From the holly print, cut:

- 1 strip, 4" x 42"; crosscut into 8 squares, 4" x 4"
- 3 strips, 1½" x 42"

From the red print, cut:

- 1 strip, 1½" x 42"; crosscut into:
  - 2 rectangles, 1½" x 8½"
  - 4 rectangles, 1½" x 4"

From the candy cane print, cut:

- 4 squares, 4" x 4"

From the green print, cut:

- 1 strip, 1½" x 42"; crosscut into:
  - 1 rectangle, 1½" x 8½"
  - 2 rectangles, 1½" x 4"

From the cream print, cut:

- 6 strips, 1½" x 42"; crosscut into:
  - 2 strips, 1½" x 26½"
  - 2 rectangles, 1½" x 10½"
  - 2 rectangles, 1½" x 8½"
  - 80 squares, 1½" x 1½"

From the red-on-red polka-dot fabric, cut:

- 6 strips, 1½" x 42"; crosscut into:
  - 38 rectangles, 1½" x 2½"
  - 76 squares, 1½" x 1½"
- 2 squares, 2⅞" x 2⅞"
- Enough 2½"-wide bias strips to make a 112" length of binding when pieced together

From the green checked fabric, cut:

- 2 strips, 2½" x 42"; crosscut into 38 rectangles, 1½" x 2½"
- 2 squares, 2⅞" x 2⅞"

Finished Quilt: 16½" x 34½"
Finished Package Block: 8" x 8"
Finished Border Block: 2" x 2"
Pieced and quilted by Cheryl Almgren Taylor.

Making the Package Blocks

1. Sew a red print 1½" x 4" rectangle between two holly print 4" squares. Press the seam allowances toward the red rectangle. Repeat to make a total of four units.

Make 4.

2. Sew a red print 1½" x 8½" rectangle between two units from step 1 to complete the block background. Press the seam allowances toward the red rectangle. Repeat to make a total of two block background squares.

Make 2.

3. Repeat steps 1 and 2 with the candy cane print squares and the green print rectangles to make one additional block background square.

4. Refer to "Fusible-Web Appliqué" on page 11 and use the patterns on page 71 to prepare the ribbon appliqués from the fabrics indicated.

5. Refer to the bow placement guide to arrange the prepared red bow appliqué pieces on the holly print block background squares and the green bow appliqué pieces on the candy cane print block background square in the order indicated. Follow the manufacturer's instructions to fuse the shapes in place.

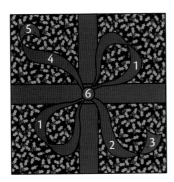

Bow placement guide

6. Finish the raw edges of each appliqué piece using a blanket stitch, zigzag stitch, or satin stitch.

Assembling the Table Runner Top

1. With the candy cane print block in the center, alternately sew the blocks and two cream 1½" x 8½" rectangles together. Be careful to orient the blocks correctly. Press the seam allowances toward the blocks. Add the cream 1½" x 26½" strips to the long edges of the joined blocks. Press the seam allowances toward the blocks. Join the cream 1½" x 10½" rectangles to the short edges of the joined blocks. Press the seam allowances toward the blocks. The table runner top must measure 10½" x 28½" or the pieced flying-geese border will not fit.

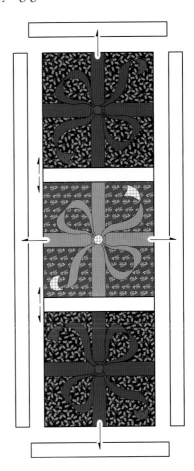

2. To make the flying-geese units for the pieced border, draw a diagonal line from corner to corner on the wrong side of each cream and each red polka-dot 1½" square.

3. Position a marked cream square on one end of each red 1½" x 2½" rectangle, right sides together. Sew on the marked line. Trim ¼" from the stitching. Press the seam allowance toward the red rectangle. Repeat on the opposite end of each rectangle, orienting the marked line as shown. Set aside the four remaining cream squares. Repeat with the red polka-dot squares and the green checked 1½" x 2½" rectangles.

Make 38.   Make 38.

4. Lay a green checked 2⅞" square on each red polka-dot 2⅞" square, right sides together. Draw a diagonal line from corner to corner on the wrong side of the green checked squares. Sew ¼" from both sides of the marked lines. Cut the squares apart on the marked line. Each pair of squares will yield two half-square-triangle units. Press the seam allowances toward the red triangles.

5. Place a marked cream square that you previously set aside on the red corner of each half-square-triangle unit. Sew on the marked lines. Cut ¼" from the stitching. Press the seam allowances toward the red fabric.

Make 4.

6. Sew 14 red-and-cream flying-geese units together side by side, joining them into pairs first. Make sure all the red points are facing the same direction. Repeat to make a total of two rows. Press the seam allowances in one direction. Repeat with the green-and-red flying-geese units, but press the seam allowances in the opposite direction as the red-and-cream units. Join the red-and-cream strip to the top

of the green-and-red strip, making sure the red and cream points are facing the same direction.

Make 2.

7. Refer to the quilt assembly diagram to sew the pieced border to the long edges of the table runner top, positioning the cream side of the strip against the cream inner border. Press the seam allowances toward the pieced borders.

8. Repeat step 6 with five red-and-cream and five green-and-red flying-geese units. Sew a unit from step 5 to each end of each strip so that the same colors butt against each other and the seam allowances match. Join these strips to the short edges of the table runner top. Press the seam allowances toward the pieced borders.

9. Refer to "Adding Borders" on page 14 to measure the table runner top for the third border. Add the holly print 1½"-wide border using the butted-corners method.

Quilt assembly

Finishing the Table Runner

1. Trim the backing fabric so that it is 4" longer and 4" wider than the table runner top.

2. Layer the backing, batting, and runner top, and baste together.

3. Quilt as desired.

4. When the quilting is complete, square up the table runner sandwich. Refer to "Binding" on page 16 to attach bias binding.

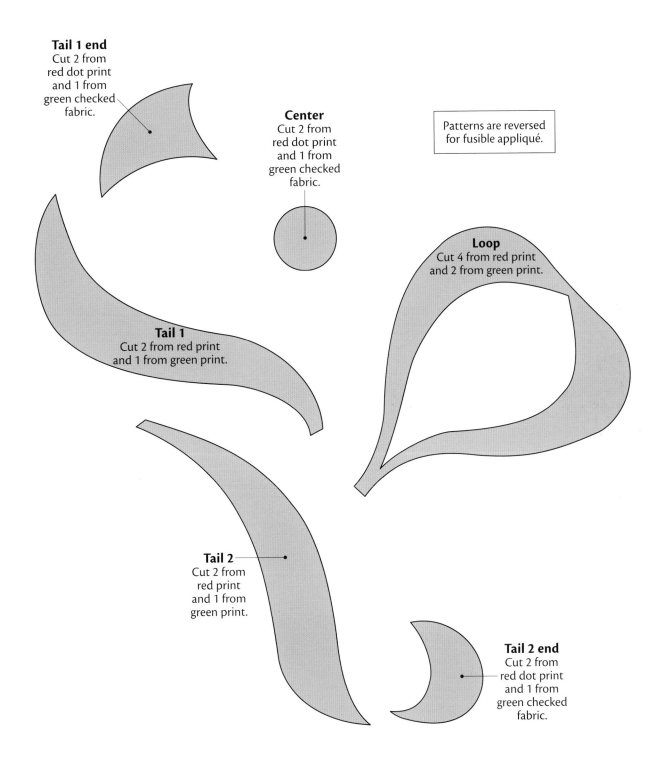

Tail 1 end
Cut 2 from red dot print and 1 from green checked fabric.

Center
Cut 2 from red dot print and 1 from green checked fabric.

Patterns are reversed for fusible appliqué.

Loop
Cut 4 from red print and 2 from green print.

Tail 1
Cut 2 from red print and 1 from green print.

Tail 2
Cut 2 from red print and 1 from green print.

Tail 2 end
Cut 2 from red dot print and 1 from green checked fabric.

TREASURED TRADITIONS

*Christmas is a time when families share memories of days
gone by while carrying special traditions into the present.
Whether the cherished activity involves hanging Christmas
stockings, baking gingerbread cookies, or kissing under
the mistletoe, any family tradition can become even
more meaningful when captured in a quilt.*

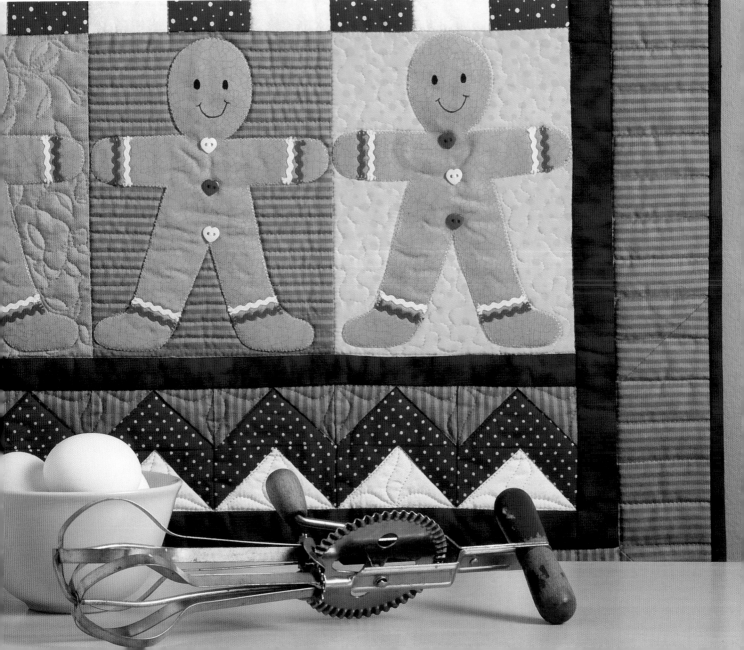

CLEONE'S CHRISTMAS STOCKING

This simple Christmas stocking is a quilted version of the one my mother, Cleone, made for me when I was very small. Every year it hung beside my sister's stocking on our fireplace. Simple and quick to make, even a beginner can sew one for a very special Christmas gift.

MATERIALS

Yardage is based on 42"-wide fabric.

⅔ yard of green print for stocking body

¼ yard of white print for cuff

Scraps of red and green fabrics for appliqués

10" x 34" piece of batting

6" length of ⅜"- to ½"-wide green double-faced satin ribbon

Green silk thread

CUTTING

From the green print, cut:

• 4 rectangles, 10" x 17"

From the batting, cut:

• 2 rectangles, 10" x 17"

MAKING THE STOCKING BODY

1. Layer two rectangles of green fabric, wrong sides together, with a batting rectangle sandwiched between the pieces. Baste the layers together. Repeat to make a total of two layered units for the stocking front and back.

2. Enlarge the pattern on page 78 to the size indicated. Using the enlarged pattern, trace the stocking onto one side of each layered unit, drawing one design in reverse. The marked line will be the stitching line. Using the silk thread, quilt the units as desired. The silk thread will give the stocking a beautiful sheen. The quilting designs on the front and back do not have to match, so be as creative as you like.

3. Cut out the front and back pieces ¼" outside the marked lines.

4. Place the front and back pieces right sides together. Sew around the pieces, ¼" from the edges, leaving the top straight edge open.

5. Fold the ribbon in half to form a loop. Place the loop on the seam line above the heel, aligning the loop ends with the top edge of the stocking. Baste the ribbon ends in place. Turn the stocking right side out.

*The back of this stocking was quilted with an elaborate
feather plume, making it reversible if desired.*

By Cheryl Almgren Taylor.

MAKING THE STOCKING CUFF

1. Using the patterns on page 79, cut two cuff front pieces and two cuff back pieces from the white print.

2. Refer to "Fusible-Web Appliqué" on page 11 and use the pattern on page 79 to prepare the holly and berry appliqués from the fabrics indicated. Refer to the cuff pattern to arrange the prepared appliqué pieces on one cuff front piece in the order indicated. Follow the manufacturer's instructions to fuse the shapes in place. Finish the raw edges of each appliqué piece using a blanket stitch, zigzag stitch, or satin stitch.

3. Sew each front piece to a back piece along one side. Press the seam allowances open. The appliquéd piece will be the outer cuff and the other piece will be the lining.

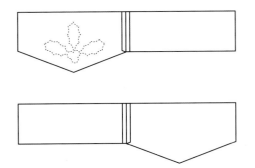

4. With right sides together, sew the cuff lining to the outer cuff along the bottom edge. Press the seam allowance toward the lining.

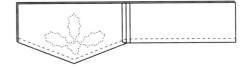

5. Sew the remaining side seams together to create a circular shape. Press the seam allowances open. The top straight edge of the cuff will still be open. Press the cuff so that the appliqué is on the outside and the seam allowances are enclosed.

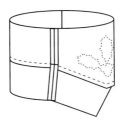

ASSEMBLING THE STOCKING

1. With right sides together, place the cuff inside the stocking, aligning the cuff raw edges with the top of the stocking. Make sure that the appliquéd side of the cuff is facing the front of the stocking and that the side seams match. Sewing from the cuff side, stitch the cuff to the stocking.

2. Pull the cuff out of the stocking and fold it over the top edge. The ribbon loop for hanging will also come out of the stocking. Press the top edge of the stocking.

Stocking
Enlarge pattern 167%.

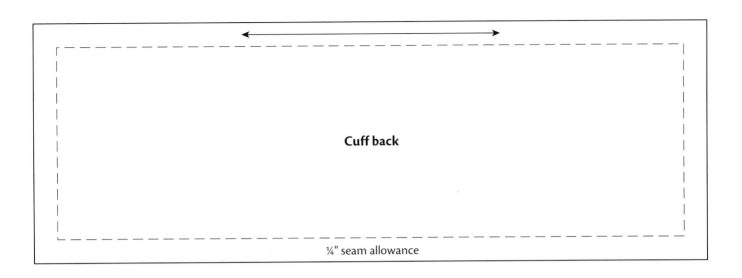

Cuff back

¼" seam allowance

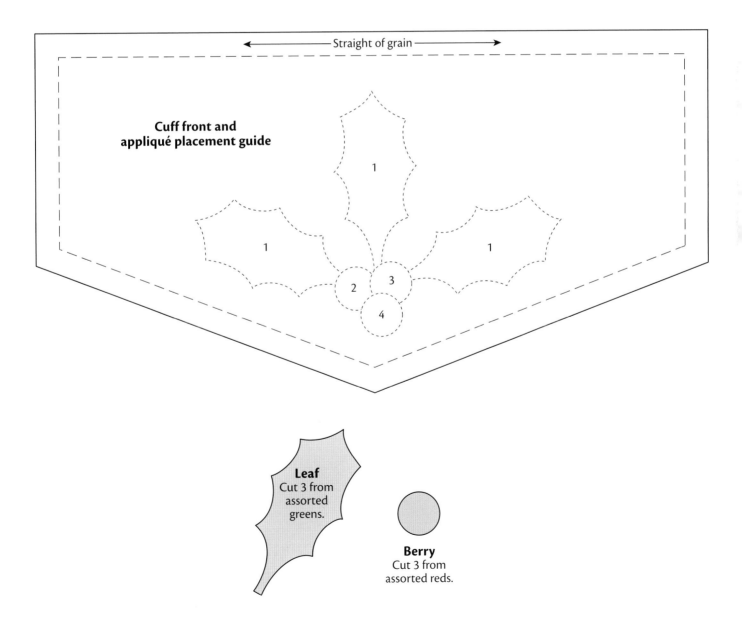

Straight of grain

**Cuff front and
appliqué placement guide**

1

1

1

2

3

4

Leaf
Cut 3 from
assorted
greens.

Berry
Cut 3 from
assorted reds.

Sweets and Treats Quilt

With its delectable candy and gingerbread men, this Christmas quilt is sure to become a family favorite, especially with children. Using a variety of green prints in the same value range adds interest to the background and provides a scrappy feel. Constructed with simple piecing and fusible appliqué, it could be the perfect project for a weekend quilting retreat.

Materials

Yardage is based on 42"-wide fabric.

1 yard *total* of assorted green prints for block backgrounds

1 yard of red print for sashing, inner border, and bias binding

¾ yard of green striped fabric for blocks, zigzag row, and outer border

½ yard of tan fabric for gingerbread man appliqués

⅜ yard of red-and-white dot print 1 for zigzag rows

¼ yard of white print for blocks, pieced sashing, and zigzag rows

⅛ yard of red-and-white dot print 2 for pieced sashing

Scraps of assorted white, red, rose, green, and yellow prints for appliqués

1⅓ yards of fabric for backing

42" x 43" piece of batting

1½ yards of red rickrack, ⅛" wide

1½ yards of white rickrack, ⅛" wide

16 red heart buttons

14 white heart buttons

Black ultra-fine-tip permanent marker

1⅛ yards of 22"-wide lightweight paper-backed fusible web

Cutting

From the assorted green prints, cut a *total* of:
- 9 rectangles, 7" x 9"
- 4 squares, 7" x 7"

From the white print, cut:
- 1 strip, 2½" x 42"; crosscut into 3 strips, 2½" x 13"
- 2 strips, 2" x 42"; crosscut into 20 rectangles, 2" x 3½"

From red-and-white dot print 2, cut:
- 1 strip, 2½" x 42"; crosscut into 3 strips, 2½" x 13"

From red-and-white dot print 1, cut:
- 4 strips, 2" x 42"; crosscut into:
  - 20 rectangles, 2" x 3½"
  - 40 squares, 2" x 2"

From the green striped fabric, cut:
- 4 strips, 3" x 42"
- 2 strips, 2" x 42"; crosscut into 40 squares, 2" x 2"
- 1 rectangle, 7" x 9"
- 1 square, 7" x 7"

From the red print, cut:
- 2 strips, 1½" x 32"
- 2 strips, 1½" x 30½"
- 2 strips, 1¼" x 30½"
- Enough 2½"-wide bias strips to make a 163" length of binding when pieced together

Finished Quilt: 37½" x 39"

Finished Gingerbread Man Block: 6" x 8"

Finished Candy Cane and Mixed Candies Blocks: 6" x 6"

Pieced and appliquéd by Cheryl Almgren Taylor;
machine quilted by Cheryl Winslow.

MAKING THE APPLIQUÉD BLOCKS

1. Refer to "Fusible-Web Appliqué" on page 11 and use the patterns on pages 86 and 87 to prepare appliqués from the fabrics indicated.

2. Use the marker to draw in each gingerbread man's eyes and mouth. Refer to the photo on page 82 and the pattern to sew red and white rickrack pieces to each gingerbread man's arms and legs.

3. Use the marker to draw the crinkle lines on the candy wrappers. Preassemble the candy canes, round candies, and oblong candies, matching the stripe pieces with the numbers on the patterns. For the oblong candies, place the green stripes on the white candy piece and the white stripes on the green candy piece.

4. Center a prepared gingerbread man appliqué on the nine assorted green print rectangles and the green striped rectangle. Follow the manufacturer's instructions to fuse the shapes in place. Refer to the Candy Cane block placement guide to arrange the prepared candy canes on two assorted green print squares and one green striped square in the order indicated, reversing the placement for one square. Fuse the shapes in place. Refer to the Mixed Candies block placement guide and the photo on page 82 to arrange the prepared round and oblong candies on the remaining green print squares, reversing the candy placement on one square. Fuse the shapes in place.

Candy Cane block placement guide

Mixed Candies block placement guide

5. Finish the raw edges of each appliqué piece using a blanket stitch, zigzag stitch, or satin stitch.

6. Square up the Gingerbread Man blocks to 6½" x 8½" and the Candy Cane and Mixed Candy blocks to 6½" square.

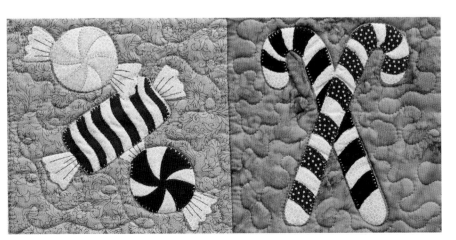

MAKING THE PIECED SASHING

1. Sew a red 2½" x 13" strip to each long edge of a white 2½" x 13" strip to make strip set A. Press the seam allowances toward the red strips. Crosscut the strip set into six segments, 1½" wide.

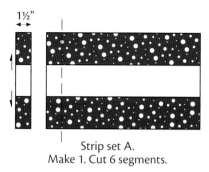

Strip set A.
Make 1. Cut 6 segments.

2. Sew a white 2½" x 13" strip to each long edge of a red 2½" x 13" strip to make strip set B. Press the seam allowances toward the red strip. Crosscut the strip set into four segments, 1½" wide.

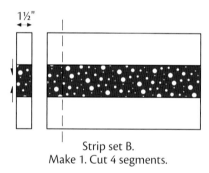

Strip set B.
Make 1. Cut 4 segments.

3. Alternately join three A segments and two B segments end to end to make a sashing strip. Repeat to make a total of two strips.

Make 2.

MAKING THE ZIGZAG ROWS

1. To make the flying-geese units for the zigzag border, draw a diagonal line from corner to corner on the wrong side of each 2" square of red-and-white dot 1 print and green striped fabric.

2. Position a marked green striped square on one end of each 2" x 3½" red-and-white dot print 1 rectangle, right sides together. Sew on the marked lines. Trim ¼" from the stitching. Press the seam allowances toward the red rectangles. Repeat on the opposite end of each rectangle, orienting the marked line as shown. Repeat with the red-and-white dot print 1 squares and the white 2" x 3½" rectangles.

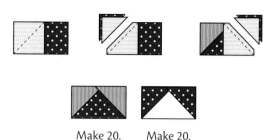

Make 20.　　Make 20.

3. Sew 10 red-and-green flying-geese units together side by side, joining them into pairs first. Make sure all the red points are facing the same direction. Repeat to make a total of two rows. Press the seam allowances in one direction. Repeat with the white-and-red flying-geese units, but press the seam allowances in the opposite direction as the red-and-green units. Join each red-and-green strip to the top of a white-and-red strip, making sure the red and white points are facing the same direction.

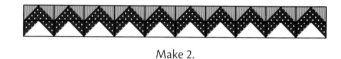

Make 2.

ASSEMBLING THE QUILT TOP

1. Refer to the photograph on page 82 and the quilt assembly diagram to arrange the Gingerbread Man blocks into two horizontal rows of five blocks each. Rearrange the Gingerbread Man blocks until you are happy with the placement of the background fabrics. Alternately arrange the Candy Cane and Mixed Candies blocks into one horizontal row, placing the reversed Candy Cane block in the center. Sew the blocks in each row together. Press the seam allowances toward the second and fourth blocks in each row.

2. Refer to the quilt assembly diagram to join the block rows, the red print 1¼" x 30½" strips, the pieced sashing strips, and the zigzag rows to complete the quilt top center.

3. Refer to "Adding Borders" on page 14 to measure the quilt top for the borders. Add the red 1½"-wide inner border using the butted-corners method, and then add the green striped 3"-wide outer border using the mitered-corner method.

FINISHING THE QUILT

1. Prepare the backing so that it is 4" longer and 4" wider than the quilt top.

2. Layer the backing, batting, and quilt top, and baste together.

3. Quilt as desired.

4. When the quilting is complete, square up the quilt sandwich. Refer to "Binding" on page 16 to attach bias binding.

5. Refer to the quilt photo and the gingerbread boy pattern to sew the heart-shaped buttons to each Gingerbread Man block, alternating the colors on each block and from block to block.

6. Add a hanging sleeve and a label to the back of your quilt.

Quilt assembly

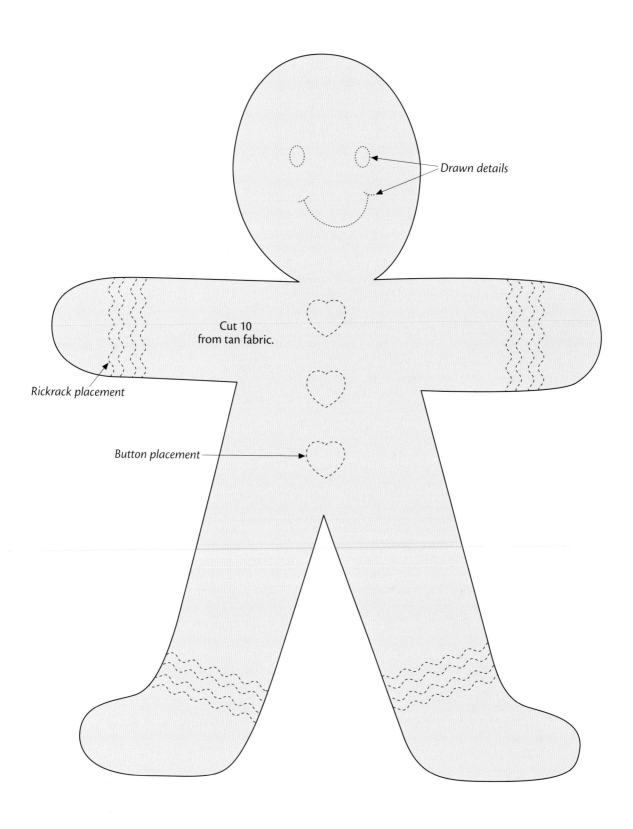

Drawn details

Rickrack placement

Button placement

Cut 10
from tan fabric.

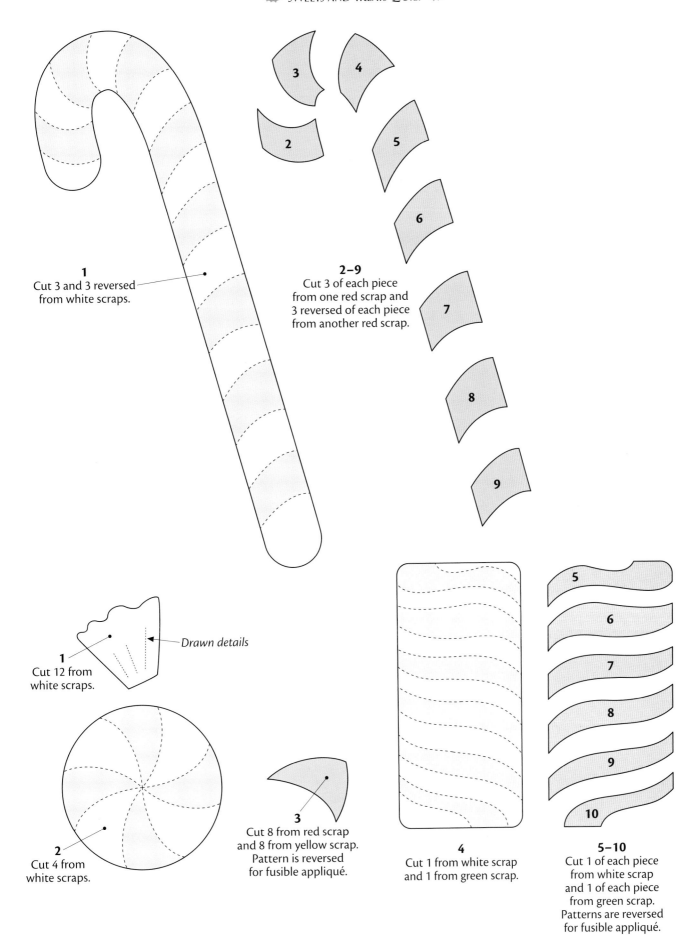

1
Cut 3 and 3 reversed
from white scraps.

2–9
Cut 3 of each piece
from one red scrap and
3 reversed of each piece
from another red scrap.

3

4

2

5

6

7

8

9

1
Cut 12 from
white scraps.

Drawn details

2
Cut 4 from
white scraps.

3
Cut 8 from red scrap
and 8 from yellow scrap.
Pattern is reversed
for fusible appliqué.

4
Cut 1 from white scrap
and 1 from green scrap.

5

6

7

8

9

10

5–10
Cut 1 of each piece
from white scrap
and 1 of each piece
from green scrap.
Patterns are reversed
for fusible appliqué.

CHRISTMAS KISSES QUILT

There's no need to hang mistletoe when you can snuggle under this Christmas quilt. The appliqué on the center blocks is embellished with tiny pearls that represent the berries, and a paper-pieced border gives the look of ribbon unfolding. The charmingly cheerful colors are sure to brighten your holiday home.

MATERIALS

Yardage is based on 42"-wide fabric.

1 yard of green dot print for inner border and bias binding

⅔ yard of white-with-red polka-dot fabric for Mistletoe and border blocks

½ yard of red-with-white polka-dot fabric for alternate blocks

⅜ yard of apple green fabric for border blocks

⅓ yard of red-and-white plaid for border blocks

⅓ yard of red-and-gold dot print for border blocks

1 fat quarter *each* of medium green and light green fabric for appliqués

1⅜ yards of fabric for backing

38" x 44" piece of batting

½ yard of 22"-wide lightweight paper-backed fusible web

Foundation paper for paper piecing

60 pearls, 4 mm

CUTTING

From the white-with-red polka-dot fabric, cut:

- 2 strips, 6½" x 42"; crosscut into 12 squares, 6½" x 6½"

- 1 strip, 3¾" x 42"; crosscut into 9 squares, 3¾" x 3¾". Cut each square once diagonally to yield 18 half-square triangles (foundation piece A).

- 1 strip, 2½" x 42"; crosscut into 15 squares, 2½" x 2½". Cut each square once diagonally to yield 30 half-square triangles (foundation piece B).

From the red-with-white polka-dot fabric, cut:

- 1 strip, 9" x 42"; crosscut into 3 squares, 9" x 9". Cut each square twice diagonally to yield 12 quarter-square triangles (you will have 2 left over).

- 1 strip, 6" x 42"; crosscut into 6 squares, 6" x 6"

- 2 squares, 4½" x 4½"; cut once diagonally to yield 4 half-square triangles

From the green dot print, cut:

- 2 strips, 2⅜" x 31½"

- 2 strips, 2¼" x 27½"

- Enough 2½"-wide bias strips to make a 157" length of binding when pieced together

Finished Quilt: 33½" x 41"
Finished Mistletoe Block: 5½" x 5½"
Finished Border Block: 3" x 3"
Pieced and quilted by Cheryl Almgren Taylor.

From the red-and-white plaid, cut:

- 3 strips, 1½" x 42"; crosscut into 22 rectangles, 1½" x 4¾" (foundation piece C)
- 1 strip, 2½" x 42"; crosscut into 10 squares, 2½" x 2½". Cut each square once diagonally to yield 20 half-square triangles (foundation piece D).

From the red-and-gold dot print, cut:

- 4 strips, 1½" x 42"; crosscut into 26 rectangles, 1½" x 4¾" (foundation piece E)
- 1 strip, 2½" x 42"; crosscut into 9 squares, 2½" x 2½". Cut each square once diagonally to yield 18 half-square triangles (foundation piece F).

From the apple green fabric, cut:

- 2 strips, 3¾" x 42"; crosscut into 13 squares, 3¾" x 3¾". Cut each square once diagonally to yield 26 half-square triangles (foundation piece G).
- 1 strip, 2½" x 42"; crosscut into 10 squares, 2½" x 2½". Cut each square once diagonally to yield 20 half-square triangles (foundation piece H).

MAKING THE MISTLETOE BLOCKS

1. Refer to "Fusible-Web Appliqué" on page 11 and use the patterns on page 93 to prepare the mistletoe appliqués from the fabrics indicated.

2. Refer to the appliqué placement guide to arrange the prepared pieces on the white-with-red polka-dot 6½" squares. Follow the manufacturer's instructions to fuse the shapes in place.

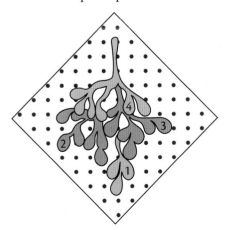

Placement guide

3. Finish the raw edges of each appliqué piece using a blanket stitch, zigzag stitch, or satin stitch.

4. Square up each block to 6" x 6".

ASSEMBLING THE QUILT TOP

1. Refer to the quilt assembly diagram on page 92 to arrange the Mistletoe blocks and the red-with-white polka-dot squares and triangles in diagonal rows. Sew the blocks and side triangles into rows. Press the seam allowances toward the red polka-dot squares and triangles. Sew the rows together, adding the corner triangles to the quilt top last. Press the seam allowances in one direction.

2. Sew the green dot 2⅜" x 31½" inner-border strips to the sides of the quilt top. Press the seam allowances toward the borders. Add the green dot 2¼" x 27½" inner-border strips to the top and bottom of the quilt top. Press the seam allowances toward the borders. The quilt top must measure 27½" x 35" or the pieced outer border will not fit.

3. Refer to "Paper Piecing" on page 13 to make copies of the paper-piecing patterns on pages 94 and 95. Make 20 copies of block A, 18 copies of block B, 2 copies *each* of blocks C and D, and 4 corner blocks. The letter after each number on the patterns correlates to the pieces in the cutting list. Use the piece listed in each area to paper piece the foundations.

4. Assemble the outer borders as shown, using the paper-pieced foundations. Match seams carefully so that the ribbon will appear to unfold across your border. Press the seam allowances of the borders as desired, except for the corner block seams, which should be pressed toward the corner blocks.

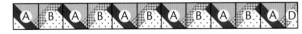

Side border.
Make 2.

Top/bottom border.
Make 2.

5. Refer to the quilt assembly diagram on page 92 to sew the side borders to the quilt top. Pay careful attention that the apple green portion of the blocks is on the outside and the white-with-red polka-dot fabric is next to the inner border. Press the seam allowances toward the inner border. Sew the top and bottom borders to the top and bottom edges of the quilt top. Press the seam allowances toward the inner border.

FINISHING THE QUILT

1. Prepare the backing so that it is 4" longer and 4" wider than the quilt top.

2. Layer the backing, batting, and quilt top, and baste together.

3. Quilt as desired.

4. When the quilting is complete, square up the quilt sandwich. Refer to "Binding" on page 16 to attach bias binding.

5. Sew 8 to 10 pearls on alternate mistletoe blocks. Randomly attach them in clusters of 2 to 4 pearls on the appliqué, giving the appearance of mistletoe berries. When attaching the pearls, go into the batting but not all the way to the backing fabric with your thread. This will firmly attach the pearls but will keep the back of your quilt looking nice.

6. Add a hanging sleeve and a label to your quilt.

Quilt assembly

Appliqué patterns are reversed
for fusible appliqué.

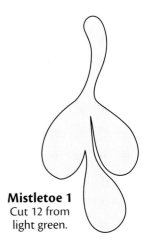

Mistletoe 1
Cut 12 from
light green.

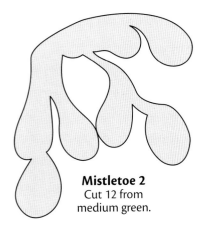

Mistletoe 2
Cut 12 from
medium green.

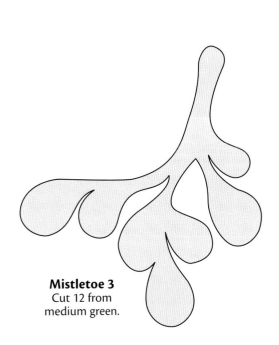

Mistletoe 3
Cut 12 from
medium green.

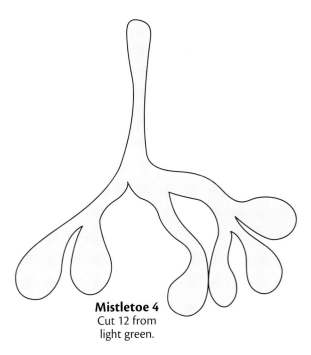

Mistletoe 4
Cut 12 from
light green.

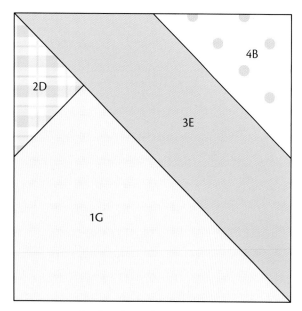

Block A foundation pattern

Block B foundation pattern

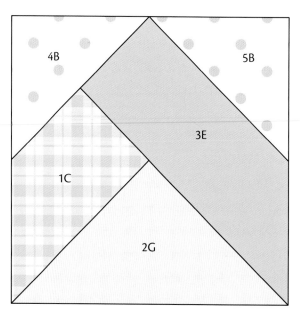

Block C foundation pattern

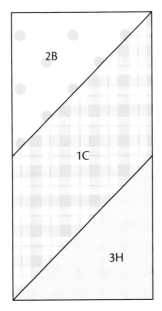

Block D foundation pattern

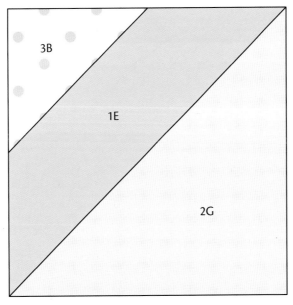

Corner Block foundation pattern

Photo by Jeffrey Herring

Family and friends are a frequent source of inspiration in my work, and
I love to see ideas come to life through the use of color, fabric, and thread.

Cheryl Almgren Taylor began her quilting career in the summer of 2000 while visiting a longtime friend, Debbie. Both had sewn since they were teenagers and had talked about learning to quilt. Because Debbie had actually taken a quilting class, she helped Cheryl get started, and they both made a quilt that week. It was the first of many for Cheryl.

Soon Cheryl was consumed with quilting and began designing her own patterns. After much encouragement from her husband and some insistence from Debbie, Cheryl submitted her designs to Martingale & Company and was thrilled when they were licensed for the pattern series *Storybook Snugglers.* Her work has also been featured in quilting magazines, and she has traveled to different parts of the United States, including an appearance at the International Quilt Festival in Houston, Texas, to lecture and teach.

Cheryl is a native Californian, transplanted to New Jersey when her husband made a career change from the oil industry to ministry. In addition to her quilting and designing, she has had a long and successful career in public education, and she currently works full time as a teacher of gifted education. She holds a BA in English literature, an MA in Curriculum and Instruction, and is certificated to teach in three states. She and her husband, Kenny, have three grown children and six grandchildren.